Dreaming of Home

To Elaine

[handwritten inscription, illegible]

Michael M[illegible]

12 [illegible] 2012

Published by
The Bible Reading Fellowship
15 The Chambers, Vineyard
Abingdon OX14 3FE
United Kingdom
Tel: +44 (0)1865 319700
Email: enquiries@brf.org.uk
Website: www.brf.org.uk
BRF is a Registered Charity

ISBN 978 1 84101 877 5
First published 2012
10 9 8 7 6 5 4 3 2 1 0
All rights reserved

Acknowledgments
Unless otherwise stated, scripture quotations are taken from The New Revised Standard
Version of the Bible, Anglicised Edition, copyright © 1989, 1995 by the Division of Christian
Education of the National Council of the Churches of Christ in the United States of America,
and are used by permission. All rights reserved.

Scripture quotations taken from the Holy Bible, New International Version, copyright © 1973,
1978, 1984, by International Bible Society. Used by permission of Hodder & Stoughton
Publishers, a member of the Hachette Livre UK Group. All rights reserved. 'NIV' is a registered
trademark of International Bible Society. UK trademark number 1448790.

Scripture quotations from THE MESSAGE. Copyright © by Eugene H. Peterson 1993, 1994,
1995. Used by permission of NavPress Publishing.

'Late Fragment' from All of Us by Raymond Carver, published by Harvill Press. Reprinted by
permission of The Random House Group Ltd.

'Heaven' by Adrian Plass, reprinted by kind permission.

Extracts from Giant's Morning Story and First Steps by Stewart Henderson are taken from A
Giant's Scrapbook published by Spire/Hodder & Stoughton 1989 and are reproduced with the
author's permission.

The paper used in the production of this publication was supplied by mills that source their
raw materials from sustainably managed forests. Soy-based inks were used in its printing and
the laminate film is biodegradable.

A catalogue record for this book is available from the British Library

Printed in Singapore by Craft Print International Ltd

Dreaming of Home

Homecoming as a model for renewal and mission

Michael Mitton

To John Hughes
Thank you for your friendship, wisdom and laughter.
Yours is a true homeward heart.

People who live this way make it plain that they are
looking for their true home.
(HEBREWS 11:14, THE MESSAGE)

Contents

❖

Foreword

The story of the prodigal son, on which this book is based, touched the very heart of Jesus' Jewish audience in the first century. Israel had been given the title of 'God's Son' throughout the narrative of the Old Testament, and, by turning their backs on God to worship man-made idols, they began a journey away from home, eventually finding themselves in exile in Babylon. By the time of Jesus, although the Jews had returned to their homeland, they were still in a state of oppression, being ruled over by the Romans. They had come home in part, at least geographically, but they longed for something more. They longed to be reconciled to their Father, to experience his love, blessing and embrace, and to enjoy the feast that they believed would accompany the arrival of God's kingdom. The story of the prodigal son is one of the many ways in which Jesus declares, 'That time has come.'

However, this story of 'God's Son' leaving home is more than just a retelling of Israel's wandering into exile; it is also a story of humanity's journey away from home. Humanity was created in the image and likeness of God, and, in light of the fact that Genesis 5:3 states that Adam had a son, Seth, in his 'image and likeness', the clear implication seems to be that what Seth is to Adam, humanity is to God: a beloved Son. Humanity was even given a beautiful home called Eden where they could live in perfect union with God and one another. We probably know how the rest of the story goes. Humanity chooses to listen to the voice of the serpent, and begins this journey into exile. Like the prodigal son contemplating dinner with the pigs, the effects of humanity's sin are dehumanising. Adam and Eve, and you and I, begin to settle for less than our true God-given identity.

Dreaming of Home brilliantly captures our desperate longings for that place called home where we know we'll experience love, safety and fullness of life. Ever since our departure from Eden, it's something we've craved. Even when Israel were in Babylon, the prophets would regularly speak not just of returning to Jerusalem, but of returning to Eden. This was clearly more than just about land and national identity; this represented a longing to discover what it truly meant to be human and to be at home with God and one another.

Over the last few years, my wife and I have been on an adventure of planting a church in central London with a particular aim of engaging in mission with a generation that, by and large, are giving up on church. A significant proportion of our church have been shaped by a postmodern worldview, are suspicious of organised religion, and doubt that church or Christianity could be of any interest or use in their life. However, they are unashamedly interested in spirituality, recognising that this journey home is very much a spiritual journey.

The sense of not feeling at home is perhaps one of the distinguishing features of postmodernism. In his book, *Picking Up the Pieces: Can Evangelicals Adapt to Contemporary Culture?*, David Hilborn states:

It is important to understand that the 'post' in 'postmodernism' is more than just chronological. It expresses, rather, a sense of leaving something behind—of moving away from something intellectually, culturally and emotionally, even though that something may stick around for some time. A useful metaphor for this is the metaphor of leaving home.

In my experience, children of postmodernity, having left home, are now longing to find a home that will be a place of healing, a place of love and peace, and also a place that provides a base camp for life's adventures. When people don't find such a home, they search for pale imitations: relationships in which they hope to find healing, jobs in which they hope to find purpose, and experiences they hope will satisfy their insatiable thirsts for contentment. When these things fail, creating further disappointment and disillusionment, the pain is numbed through the self-medication of drink, drugs, workaholism, sexaholism and other addictions. People are crying out for a safe place to process their pain. They are desperate to find a home in which to heal.

This predicament, while tragic, provides an exciting opportunity for the gospel. People are hungry to find such a home, and the message we have been entrusted with is that relationship with Jesus, and the authentic and adventurous community known as his body, the church, is the home that satisfies our greatest desires and longings.

Reading *Dreaming of Home*, I regularly found myself weeping both for myself and for the people our church is trying to reach in central London. There are areas in my own life where I feel a long way from home, and, through reading this book, I felt God reach such places, embrace me, and lovingly remind me that it's time to come home. At the same time, I felt two further challenges: firstly to proclaim this great news to those searching, that in Christ all our homeward longings are fulfilled, and secondly to make our church a genuine home for such people: a place to heal, to find life, to find love, and to find adventure.

I couldn't recommend this book more highly. It contains a critical message for the church today in how to engage with culture, and particularly those who are spiritually searching for 'home'. But for more than just his message, I couldn't recommend Michael more highly as a person. He has such a deep intimacy with God that in his presence my strivings are gently quietened, and I'm reminded afresh of the central truths that I'm loved, accepted, and called by God into the most exciting of adventures.

For those reading this book, you're in for such an encounter. A feast awaits you, and on the menu in *Dreaming of Home* is an invitation to embark on a journey towards authenticity and adventure: a journey home to the Father's embrace where fullness of life awaits.

Pete Hughes, Team Leader, Kings Cross Church (KXC), London

Introduction

If I were allowed to travel in time to any moment of my choice, I know where I would like to go. I would ask to be taken to a hillside, as I imagine it, somewhere on a warm sunny afternoon in first-century Palestine. I have slipped away from work early to join a crowd of others who have gathered because they have heard that there is a rabbi in town who has become well known for his wise words and extraordinary miracles. I imagine myself to be in that place of knowing little of the story of this man and yet having an instinct that tells me I need to listen to him, and listen to him with all I've got and for all I'm worth. So, using my height to see above the heads in front of me, I catch sight of him sitting on a dusty wall in the shade of a fig tree. I see his hands gesturing and his eyebrows rising and falling as he tells the captive group story after story, and I see on the faces of his onlookers expressions of concern, amusement, puzzlement, delight, and in the eyes of some I catch sight of moisture before it is hastily brushed away in embarrassment.

I listen—in a way I seldom listen, as if my life depends on what I hear. I hear a story I know so well in this present age, and yet in my time travelling I am hearing it as it was told for the first time and so it is completely new to me. The young rabbi shifts his body and now faces me and catches my eye, only momentarily but enough for me to know that he has noticed me and I am included in this group of people whom he is addressing. Here, in this particular place in this time that I have chosen to visit, he has a story to tell, a story that will be talked about for more than 2000 years after its first telling. And he begins, 'There was a man who had two sons...'

We are away and I sense I am not the only one who, as the story unfolds, has a keen and unnerving sense that this is a story that has been written just for me. It's not that I have had a life of stealing my inheritance, dashing off to far-off lands, spending everything on wine, women and song and coming back with my tail between my legs. It's not me, and yet, disturbingly and wonderfully, there is something in this story that is exactly me, and he knows it and I know it. I know it is me, because when he gets to the end and says, 'and the father ran out to him and hugged and kissed him and said, "Welcome home"', I am aware that the 'prodigal' part of me is a far greater part than I once thought.

The parables of Jesus must have been extraordinarily powerful when they were first delivered by Jesus as he criss-crossed that ancient land, making his pilgrim way to Jerusalem. Yet, despite the passing of time and the very different culture of 21st-century Britain, this parable of the prodigal son is as compelling and contemporary as ever. You would think that a story of this sort would have a limited life: you could give a few years to approaching it from different angles, and if you went at it long enough you would get all the meat of it and it would then be fairly useless. And yet, as I approach it again, it seems to have more meat on it than ever, and if ever there are multiplication miracles it is in the way these parables go on feeding us year after year without diminishing. The prodigal son story, as it is traditionally called, is one of the best loved and best known of the parables and is a story where the punchline is to do with coming home. When I allow it to speak to me, I find this simple story, more than any other, makes me aware that within my soul there is a yearning to come home, and it is one of the deepest yearnings of my life. I am discovering that I am not alone in this quest.

The Irish nun Sister Stan, in her book *Now is the Time*, writes:

We all need to come home. We have a place that we can call home and we need to belong to a society and culture. We need to be at home within our own hearts. We need to find a home in the hearts of others; and we need to be at home with our God. The journey home for all of us is different, longer or shorter, physically, socially, emotionally, spiritually. Our whole life is that journey home, the journey from home to home, threshold to threshold.[1]

Some time ago, I took a three-month sabbatical. In the year leading up to it, I became disturbed by these words of Sister Stan, because I was aware of a gnawing fact that I was not yet at home in myself. I became aware of a yearning to be at home in my own heart, and I knew there were thresholds I had yet to cross. This conviction was enhanced by a night-time dream about six months before my sabbatical. It was a dream that I realised was so full of meaning that I had to get hold of it, understand its language and get its message. To help me with this task I booked in with a counsellor and met with her each week of my sabbatical. It turned out that every part of the dream held significance for me and, in listening to this voice that spoke to me from just below the surface of my conscious life, I made progress towards finding a home in my heart. In discovering this home, I became clearer about who I am and my own vocation, and that in turn became the catalyst for taking one of the biggest risks of my life, which was to come out of paid employment and to launch out into a freelance ministry.

As I write this I find myself remembering a very good friend who died more than ten years ago and whom I still miss greatly. Brother Ramon SSF was a Franciscan hermit who was known and loved by many people. I used to visit him in his little hermitage at Glasshampton monastery, which is set in beautiful Worcestershire fields. Ramon lived his hermit life in a group of small huts set in an orchard just beyond the monastery vegetable garden. I remember my visits to him very clearly: I would make my way down past the runner beans and raspberries, ring the bell by the gate and enter the orchard. Out would come the beaming Ramon and, with hugs and laughter, he would welcome me into his home for a cup of tea and hours of animated conversation that would include theology, philosophy, stories, poetry, songs, tears, laughter, prayer and silences. The thing I admired about Ramon was that he was one who was indeed at home in himself and I found his to be a most hospitable home.

Sadly, Ramon became ill with a cancer that eventually took him from us. In his last months he moved out of his airy hermitage into a room in the monastery. On one of the last occasions I visited him he was lying in bed and, though ailing in body, he was very strong in his spirit. At one point, during a conversation in which he was trying to help me understand a complicated piece of mystical theology (which took some doing), he paused and, pulling himself up, leaned towards me and said in his deep, lyrical, Welsh voice, 'You see the trouble with you, Michael, is that you have not yet become Michael Mitton', and the echo of that prophetic insight has resounded in my soul ever since. What he was in effect saying was that I was not yet at home in my own heart, and thus had not yet become who I was born to be. I think my hope had been that somehow or other I would in time become myself, just through the normal process of living. But I came to the realisation that this wasn't happening of its own accord, and I had to do something to enable me to become Michael Mitton! It was during my sabbatical that I made significant progress, and I think if you were to meet me now there would be a very reasonable chance that you would meet someone who is well on his way to becoming Michael Mitton, for little by little I am discovering who I am.

I know I am not alone in the need to become at home in myself. In the six years that I worked in the training department of Derby Diocese I spent many hours in the company of clergy and lay people who were doing their best to serve Christ faithfully in a church and world of persistent pressures and rapid change. From time to time I have seen something of the pain and alienation that lie behind well-developed defences, and I have found myself with that tell-tale lump in the throat when I see those defences give way, betrayed by the watery signs of human fear and trembling, doubt and sorrow. At those moments I can see evidence that my friends are feeling a kind of homesickness and, to use the poignant language of Psalm 137, are struggling to sing the Lord's song in a foreign land. Once or twice I have imagined that if they were to start their morning service with a song that declared where they honestly found themselves at this point in life, rather than intoning some opening responses, they might well stand up and sing, probably with a shaky, uncertain voice, Paul Simon's 'American Tune', which talks about how we can't expect to be bright and cheerful when we are far away from home.

It is seeing the signs of being far away from home in my own soul, and in the hearts and minds of those with whom I have been working, that has caused me to develop a determination to find out how we can make our way home. In fact, as I've gone on, I have come to believe that finding the way home may be the only way to make sense of a world where we struggle against confusion, forsakenness and deep weariness.

The subject of home sounds straightforward. In fact, it sounds quite interesting but not particularly exciting. Plenty of people have written books with the word 'home' in their titles, so there is nothing new about it. It seems reasonably safe, nothing too contentious, and generally speaking like familiar ground, for we have all come from homes and live in homes. But, as I have explored this subject, I have found that I am on anything but familiar ground and in territory that is certainly not well defined. I thought that the theme of home would conjure up images of family groups resting by firesides on winter evenings, but instead I found that I was in a far more chilling world of head-on encounters with fears and shames and shadow sides and longings, and only by facing these have I found the road home. For myself, the exploration has been far from safe, and yet wonderfully rewarding.

So here I am embarking on another book as if I am an expert on the subject. I never have been an expert and never intend to be. I am committed to being an amateur, not least because I like the fact that an amateur does something for love—the word is derived from the first word I learned in Latin: *amo*, 'I love'. I am an amateur who is trying to love his way home because I instinctively know that home is the place where I can get my bearings, and if I can get those then I can go anywhere in this world, including the inner world of my own soul. I am writing this book because I hope that, by sharing the experience and insights that I have gathered along the way, those who read it will also be helped in finding their way home. In the following pages I shall look at the meaning of 'home' and the host of feelings associated with that powerful word, and I shall also look at how we can adventure into our own souls, examining ways of becoming more at home in these lives that have been entrusted to us during our time on earth. I am also interested in the notion that church is home, and how for many who feel emotionally and spiritually homeless in our turbulent world this is good news indeed. As you would expect, the book will end with some thoughts about our final home that we call heaven. From time to time I shall go back to Galilee and listen to that story of the father and his sons and try to garner some of the wealth of insights about homecoming contained in that story, which is as alive for us today as it was when it was first told.

Finally, I shall do with this book what I have done with two others of mine, and that is to run alongside the main text a fictional story. It is simply another way of getting the message across, though the beauty of stories is that they engage the imagination, and in that way give you more room to explore the themes. This time I am writing a story around the prodigal son parable, and I shall pick up where I started this introduction, by taking us back in time to that day when the parable was first told. I have invented a character, a Pharisee called Reuben. I had no idea how this parable would affect him as I started to write but I found his story came to light in the course of the writing.

As I have already mentioned, for very good reasons this parable is one of the best-known in the Gospels. At one level, there is very little more to be said about it. But, as I have been working with this theme of home in talks and seminars with different groups in different parts of the country, again and again I find myself being drawn back to this parable as if it is deliberately trying to catch my attention. When I return to it, I feel like someone who is looking at the same view for the umpteenth time yet knows he is missing something obvious. To write about the parable in this fictional story is my way of trying to spot aspects of the story that I have previously missed through my familiarity with it. I hope that, if nothing else, it will cause you to dig deeper into the story and discover your own treasures.

For those who find such things helpful, I have included some questions for reflection at the end of each chapter. These questions may not be right for you, but they may give you a starting point to help you find your questions, and give you space to reflect on your own journey home.

So the book is about to get under way. You bring to this book your own unique experience of life; you have chosen to read this particular book at this particular time perhaps because something in you hankers after home. Over the years I have become convinced that every life is of infinite value to our Father in heaven, who gets concerned even when a sparrow has sung its last song and falls to the ground (Matthew 10:29). Not only is every life of value, but every part of life. Some people seem to live lives full of high drama and heroism and startling miracles that take your breath away, but most of us get through the majority of our days with breath intact and without exceptional things happening. Yet I am coming to recognise that every day is actually full of exceptional happenings if only we have the eyes to see and the ears to hear. Imagine Moses all those days in the wilderness shuffling through the dust and dodging the sheep muck, and scratching his ankles and feet on the desert shrubs. Every day, desert shrub after desert shrub, until one day the shrub was ablaze with the glory of God and his scratched feet kicked off their sandals because the desert sand had become the gold dust of holy ground. Maybe the desert was full of the fire of God every day, but on this particular day, for reasons that Moses probably never knew, he had the eyes to see the blazing shrub and the ears to hear the call of God and the feet to stand on holy ground, and as a result a people were led home.

There are fiery signs pointing to our homeland all over this world. Our task is to be on the lookout in the everyday and ordinary stuff of our lives. So pause and pray that God will touch the eyes of your heart so that through these ordinary pages of print, held alongside your unique experience of life, you will find your own piece of holy ground and catch sight of the fire that is a message for you, a waymark to your homeland.

Dedication

I have dedicated this book to John Hughes. When people are ordained they are placed in a parish with a more senior vicar whose task it is to show them the ropes of parish life and send them on their way after about four years, so they can be a vicar themselves, and it was John who was my training vicar after I was ordained at the age of 25. At that time John was Vicar of St Andrew's Church, High Wycombe, and in the early weeks of settling into my life as a curate it became clear that John and I were very much on the same wavelength. I immediately respected him for his wisdom and bold leadership, but more than anything I was grateful to him for offering me such a deeply human, as well as deeply spiritual, model of leadership. We would laugh ourselves into helplessness on many occasions, and we would also weep together at the sadnesses and tragedies we encountered in pastoral ministry. We prayed together and knew the power of God together. Thankfully our friendship did not end with that curacy, and over the years I have often gone to John for his guidance. I visited him during my time of exploring this theme of home on my sabbatical, and typically he had such a clear prophetic word for me, borne from his listening heart, that it has become a prominent landmark on my journey home. I am one of many who owe him such a depth of gratitude.

I am also grateful to John's wife Annie, who made me so welcome in those early days in Wycombe, and I felt so honoured when they asked me to be godfather to their second son, Peter. I have loved Pete from the moment I first saw him at only a day or two old, and I have followed his journey into a pioneering ministry with great admiration. I am so grateful to him for writing the foreword to this book. His conviction that the theme of home has a powerful message for his generation reassures me that my interest in the subject is not just my way of handling mid-life crisis but that home is a theme of relevance to all generations!

Reuben's story (1)

I had no intention of stopping that afternoon. It was not long before the sun set and the Sabbath preparations began. Like my fellow Pharisee friends, I am always busy because the people need so much help, and it is in my nature to help. My beloved wife, Ruth, always says, 'It's time you stopped helping them, Reuben. You'll help yourself into an early grave if you go on like this!' It is not my fault—the Almighty made me that way, and he gives me the Sabbath each week and on that holy day I rest deeply.

So it was the end of my working week and, though I am young and healthy, I felt weary. The sun had been very hot on this particular day as I was walking home. I was not far from my house when I saw a crowd gathered around the so-called Rabbi from Galilee. He had been in these parts for a little while, and we had become accustomed to him, but none of us liked him and he clearly had no regard for us—so we thought. He seemed to do things deliberately to annoy us, like working on the Sabbath. That was one of his favourites. You can't imagine how angry it made us. It was so confusing for the people! We had done our utmost to teach them what they may and may not do on the Sabbath, working it out to the finest detail so that they wouldn't get it wrong. So, when I saw him sitting on a wall in the shade of a large fig tree, I instinctively felt irritated by him and, even though I did not want to hear his heresies, I felt I should go to protect the people. Someone, some figure of authority, needed to be there to correct his false teaching. I felt tired, and Ruth needed me at home, but my sense of duty got the better of me.

I was glad to see that my old friend Shemaiah was also there, but, as far as I could make out, we were the only two Pharisees in that particular crowd. There were a few foolish Sadducees as well, I noticed, who were looking stern-faced as usual, as they watched the Rabbi. I made my way towards the front of the crowd so I could hear what the upstart Galilean was saying. I also wanted to be near Shemaiah for strength in numbers in combating the heretical teaching. Shemaiah was older and far wiser than me, and so committed. He and my father loved to argue about very fine points of the law. I'm not as clever as either of them, and I would sit back and keep quiet, admiring their amazing minds.

When I got within hearing distance, I heard the Rabbi telling one of his stories—it always annoyed us that he kept telling these stories. Why couldn't he just come clean about what he believed and tell it to us straight? It seemed so devious. It was as if he had something to hide. As I realised later, it was more because we had something to find.

He was telling the people a story about a woman who had lost a coin and somehow he managed to use it to tell us that we needed to repent. He was clearly having a dig at Shemaiah and me when he said that. Then he started up another story, one that at first sounded so outrageous and so offensive that I thought I would throw something at him. But, while most of me was raging, there was another bit of me that became full of curiosity, even wonder, and it was that bit which crept out from some hidden part of my soul that afternoon and caught sight of a world I didn't dare believe existed.

He paused quite a long time before he began this story, looking round the crowd. Some of the crowd were sitting on the dusty ground, and some stood, trying to find little bits of shade, as the sun was still hot. Just before he spoke, a woman handed him a cup of water, which he drank gratefully, and he used the last drops to wipe his face, so that for a moment or two it shone disturbingly. The branches of the fig tree laden with hard unripe fruit swayed in a welcome breeze, and the dappled light flickered over his glistening face as he looked out over the crowd. He sat still for a moment, then drew in a long breath and said, 'There was a man who had two sons', and in that opening moment I thought this might at last be a good story with nothing contentious in it. But I was wrong.

He continued, 'The younger son said to his father, "Father, give me a share of the estate."' Well, you could hear the gasps of shock around the crowd. In all my years I have never heard of such a thing. Wealthy or poor, all fathers we have ever known would *never* give away their inheritance before they died. I know my father could get very angry, and there were, I am ashamed to say, times when my anger towards him burned in my heart, but never did it occur to me to wish him dead! The thought was utterly appalling. How could this Galilean Rabbi put such ideas into the people's minds? It was bad enough having the Zealots stirring up the people to violence against the Romans, but to evoke such feelings of violence in the home against fathers was utterly outrageous. I looked at Shemaiah, wondering if we should find a way of stopping this man. He looked grim-faced, but held his hand up to stop me taking any action. 'Give him a chance—let him complete the story,' he whispered.

The Rabbi continued, and horrified us again by saying that the father actually *agreed* to the son's request and *gave* him his

20

inheritance there and then. What kind of a father would be so weak as to do that? I thought of my own father and imagined what would have happened if I had asked for my share of the inheritance. I could see it in my mind's eye: his red face and bulging eyes, his fury, his huge fist hammering the table, his swearing, the smell of sweat and wine; his telling me to leave the home, just as he did to my older sister on that dreadful day 15 years ago. Come to think of it, it was the kind of thing Judith might have done if women received the inheritance. But not me—I was the one my father could rely on. I would never say a word against him. I might not have had many brains, as he often pointed out, but I was completely loyal. To have asked for my inheritance? Can you imagine that?

All these thoughts filled my mind, and he had only just got started on the story. Somehow or other his few words had had the effect of opening a kind of trapdoor into the cellar of my soul, where I kept hidden my private thoughts and my hopes and fears. Now the afternoon sunlight lit them up—my father, his anger, my anger, my fears, my beliefs. As the story went on, I was to discover that there was much more in that cellar than I had ever imagined. Not least, there was a whole collection of longings that I had not looked at since childhood.

The sun flickered through the leafy branches. I breathed in, anxiously, for I felt danger in the air. And yet something about the expression on this Rabbi's face told me that only if I *failed* to listen to this story would I be in real danger. So I listened, and I joined that son in his journey to the far-off land.

—— Chapter 1 ——

The homing instinct

The day I set about writing this chapter I received an email from Rowland Evans, who is a remarkable Welsh visionary, writer and missionary who not long ago passed his 70th birthday and typically celebrated it with a church-planting and teaching visit to China. In his email describing the visit, he ends with these words: 'The deepest dream of human longing is to belong, to find a place of unconditional acceptance where we can be at home. We will recognise that place, for it is where God stands for each of us.'[2]

Rowland would know the Welsh word *hiraeth*, a word unknown to me until recently, but when I discovered it I instinctively warmed to it. I trawled the Internet, looking for references to the word, and on one site I found that a Welshman now living in Canada defined it in this way:

Hiraeth *(pronounced 'hee-rah-y-th') is a Welsh word which has no single-word equivalent in English. It implies a wistful longing, interwoven with homesickness, with overtones of happiness for fond memories of happy times that once were, tinged with sadness (even tears) because they are no more, plus an aching emptiness and some heartache too, all rolled together into a painfully deep, gut-wrenching yearning.*

Interviewed in the *Guardian*,[3] the Welsh baritone Bryn Terfel was asked, 'What one song would feature on the soundtrack of your life?' and he answered, 'One I've sung called "My Little Welsh Home". There's a word in Welsh, *hiraeth*, which is all about longing. Travelling performers and businessmen are all like little birds wanting to fly home.'

I find the whole business of birds flying home utterly extraordinary. A few weeks before I wrote this, I took a walk along the Tissington Trail (a former railway line) in my Derbyshire homeland on a very cold day in the middle of February. At one point I left the trail and walked over some fields and came to a small ruined farm building, and there, stuffed into the weathered rafters, was a small, compact and beautifully constructed swallow's nest, decorated with tiny ice crystals. For a moment I was caught by a sense of wonder as I thought of the owner of this nest, a swallow in the warm climes of South Africa that was very likely, at this moment, to be starting to get itchy wings. Something would be stirring in its breast, a restlessness, a wistful longing, a memory, a need, an overwhelming desire to travel north. Any day now the longing would become so strong that it would set off on its journey. If it was one of the fit and experienced swallows, it would cover an astonishing 200 miles per day, crossing mountains, deserts, cities and seas, and through some quite extraordinary instinctive satnav system make its way to this little Derbyshire nest.

In the first chapter I mentioned Sister Stan. Her full name is Sister Stanislaus Kennedy and she is a member of the Sisters of Charity. She hails originally from County Kerry, but has spent much of her working life among the homeless in Dublin, co-founding the homelessness charity Focus Ireland. In her book of daily readings, she chose to write this for the reading for Christmas Day:

Those without a home feel it very deeply at Christmas. There are people who pretend they go home at this time of year rather than admit to themselves or others that they have no home to go to. Home is the place where we discover who we are, where we are coming from and where we are going to. It is where we are helped to establish our own identity. It is where we learnt to love and be loved. It is where our needs of the mind, body and spirit are first recognized and met. It is where we learn to become whole, stable and yet always open to change and surprise.[4]

Her work with people who have no home has given her a keen sensitivity to the fundamental need in all of us to find somewhere we can call home. It is more than a roof over our heads—she is alerting us to the fact that it is a place of belonging and provides an environment in which we discover just who we are in this often bewildering world. It is a place that gives us the security to become open to change and surprise.

Childhood home

In any thinking about home we will sooner or later find our minds drawn back to our childhood homes. The American novelist and Presbyterian minister Frederick Buechner, in his book *The Longing for Home*, writes:

To think about home eventually leads you to think back to your childhood home, the place where your life started, the place which off and on throughout your life you keep going back to if only in dreams and memories and which is apt to determine the kind of place, perhaps a place inside of yourself, that you spend the rest of your life searching for even if you are not aware that you are searching.[5]

For some, to think of their childhood home will evoke warm and comforting memories; for others, quite the reverse; and for most of us there will be a fair mix of happy, sad, comforting, frightening, exciting and disturbing and much more. When my children were small, we holidayed one year in Scotland and stopped the night in Edinburgh before travelling further north. I decided to take them to see the house where I was born in Morningside, and we drove down Cluny Gardens, the road that was once so familiar to me, and I parked the car opposite number 30. We all got out of the car and stood on the pavement looking at the stone-built, sturdy, semi-detached house, and I proudly presented my childhood home. As you can imagine, the response was 'Can we go now?' because the only person for whom this house had special relevance was me. Home is very personal.

It was in this house that, on one cold March day, I arrived in the upstairs bedroom. As the midwife wrapped me in towels, I gasped for breath, while my mother gasped for her Craven A cigarettes, which she always gave up during her pregnancies but delighted to return to once the baby was delivered. I found myself to be not only in a smoky house but a crowded one at that, with a mother, father, brother and three sisters. For seven years I lived in that home until the family moved south to Buckinghamshire, where I remained for the rest of my childhood.

As I think back to those childhood years in Edinburgh, I recall a great difference between the world inside home and the one beyond it. Inside the house that was my home, the world was safe, secure and happy; but venturing outside always involved risk, and, for reasons I have never fully understood, the world beyond home was one that held many fears, made up of a great assortment of threats, including the large dog in the house opposite, the searing screech of the dentist's drill, the cold steel syringes that delivered painful polio inoculations, and the angry shouts of the primary school headmistress.

In this respect, I have always felt some affinity with John Betjeman, who writes about his experience of home so movingly in his *Summoned By Bells*. I particularly love the televised version of this long autobiographical poem of his journey through childhood into adulthood. At one point we see him standing outside his old childhood home, 31 West Hill in Highgate, North London. As usual he is looking dishevelled with his shirt breaking free from his trousers, his jacket button straining to hold everything together, and his corduroy peaked cap pressed hard on to his wispy white hair. But there he is in the front garden of the house he loved so much, poking at familiar stones with his walking stick, and looking wistful. We hear his old voice reciting the poem, and in the space of just a few lines he repeatedly uses the word 'safe'.[6] He and I were fortunate. As children, home for us was indeed a place of safety.

For others, however, the experience was quite the opposite: as they look back at their childhood, home was the place of fears, and the outside world was the place to escape to for safety. For others, from what used to be called 'broken homes', there were two homes to relate to, one where Mum lived and the other where Dad lived, and experiences of each can be very different. We all carry our own unique memories and experiences, which all go to making us who we are today.

At the same time, the word 'home' won't simply throw us back in our memories to our childhood homes, for we will also think of the house we currently live in, the building we come back to, the place where we rest and from which some of us work, and the place where we may live with others who significantly contribute to this experience of home. But Frederick Buechner, in the passage I quoted above, makes me aware of another home—a home that is beyond and somehow more than the homes we have lived in. I don't think he is referring to our eternal home here, though we will come to that in due course. I believe he is referring to a longing for something like an *ideal* home.

The ideal home

There is within us a homing instinct for something more than a house or a land where we live or have lived. It is a longing for, a hankering after, this ideal home, this place of utter safety and belonging where, more than anything else, we can be ourselves without fear or shame. This is a longing that we do well to attend to, and it is my experience that by attending to it I have discovered something about living more fully in the life that has been entrusted to me. We all have parts of us that are too sheltered, that are afraid to come out for one reason or another. If bits of us are hiding away like this, it is a clue that we are not yet entirely at home in ourselves—there are forces that prevent us from being fully ourselves.

In Bible stories of human encounters with the divine, very often the response of those humans is either to be very afraid, like the shepherds with the angels (Luke 2:9), or to feel deeply ashamed, like Isaiah when he saw the Lord high and lifted up in the temple (Isaiah 6:5). The chances are that if you or I were suddenly to be visited by an angel today, we would either feel full of fear or we would become aware of our failings and sinfulness, and thereby feel ashamed. But it is not just an angelic encounter that may have this effect on us. How many of us find safe places in this world, where we can honestly say we feel free to be fully ourselves? To own up honestly to being truly who we are—including what we believe or don't believe, what we feel or don't feel, what is going through our minds, our private thoughts and imaginings—carries great risk. To do so might provoke anger or aggression of some kind, or it may provoke rejection or ridicule. And rather than risk this, we keep such parts of ourselves under wraps, offering only what it feels safe to share. Of course, it would hardly be appropriate to wear our hearts on our sleeves the whole time, but for many of us the problem is that our hearts rarely make it anywhere near our sleeves.

There is also the difficulty of admitting some of our fears, struggles and longings even to ourselves. We struggle to get our heart on to our sleeve even in private. This just adds to the distancing of ourselves from our true homeland, that safe place where we can kick off our shoes and be utterly free and relaxed. Even when we start to admit to aspects of our personality that we prefer to keep hidden, we may find that within us is a censoring voice that disapproves of what it sees, and so our 'real' self flees back under cover again.

When I was starting to explore this subject, I happened to be visiting family on the south coast of Ireland, and on a bright and breezy September day I wandered into a ramshackle little book-shop in Kinsale where I came across John O'Donohue's book *Benedictus*. I sat down in one of the comfy armchairs in the shop and discovered the book had a section on homecomings. I don't know of many who had such a way with words as John O'Donohue had, and typically he was able to put into words what I was beginning to feel:

Home is where the heart is. It stands for the sure centre where individual life is shaped and from where it journeys forth. What it ultimately intends is that each of its individuals would develop the capacity to be at home in themselves. This is something that is usually overlooked but is a vital requirement in the creativity and integrity of individual personality... When one is at home in oneself, one is integrated and enjoys a sense of balance and poise. In a sense that is exactly what spirituality is: the art of homecoming. [7]

In reading this, I realised that homecoming is in many respects another name for spirituality. Some have presented spirituality as the kind of thing we get into to escape from our normal, worldly, unspiritual self. True spirituality, however, is daring to discover the real us, including the normal, earthy, unspiritual bits, and to explore the life of the Spirit in a place that is authentically us.

In the beginning

One of the reasons why the opening two chapters of Genesis are so comforting is that they depict a situation in which two humans are utterly at home in the kind of way I have been describing. In Genesis 2 we get the second account of the creation, where the writer tells us something very important about the relationship between God and humans. In this account, after he has created the cosmos that includes this planet Earth, God puts his mind to forming humans. Put aside for one moment all anxieties to do with Darwin, evolution and dinosaurs and let the writer take you into the key message of this story. Here is the Lord God caring for this beautiful creation constructed by his heart and his hand. The earth may not yet have any sophisticated form of life, but deep within it there is life in the form of water (v. 6). There is movement in this world, something is stirring in her—she is starting to give birth and, to keep with the language of birth, her waters break as streams come up from deep within her and make their way to the surface of this brand new planet, heralding the emerging of new life. In this account, before he gets round to making any other creatures, God scoops his hand into the yielding earth, and, for reasons that are left to our imagination, he decides to make a creature that is alive with his own breath (v. 7). This life, more than any other, will be infused with his life. He now develops a garden that is called Eden, a word that has the same meaning as paradise. He furnishes this new and perfect land with other forms of life and entrusts it all into the human's care. The man has complete freedom, except for the fact that he must not eat from the tree of the knowledge of good and evil. The result of eating of that tree would be death, a concept that is utterly alien to this paradise.

The story develops with the creation of the woman (vv. 18–24), whose life is intricately bound up with that of the man, and the writer calls them man and wife. The final verse of this brilliant chapter tells us that 'The man and his wife were both naked, and they felt no shame' (v. 25, NIV). This sentence summarises the exquisite quality of this perfect home. In their nakedness the man and woman have found a place where they can be fully and openly themselves without any fear or shame; there is nothing to hide or hide from. It is only when they do eat of the tree of the knowledge of good and evil that they experience feelings of fear and shame. They then have the power to imagine evil, and waters have broken again, this time not for life but for death as chaos enters a once-perfect world.

This storyteller gives us an endearingly human view of God, who is heard strolling through the garden in the cool of the evening (3:8). He is out looking for the couple he has created and eventually finds the man, who has now stitched together some fig leaves with which to cover himself. He says to God, 'I heard you in the garden, and I was afraid because I was naked; so I hid' (v. 10, NIV). The eating of the fruit has introduced the man to the notion of shame, and because he is ashamed, he is afraid of what God will think of him when he sees him. So he does what we all do when we are ashamed and afraid: we hide and we try covering ourselves up. Paradise is lost. From now on, humanity will have to work hard to search for a home that will be a place like paradise, a world free of these two imprisoning powers of shame and fear. However, hard though it may be to find, humans never lose the instinct to long for that home. They are like the swallows crossing deserts and seas, knowing that this place of belonging does exist where they can arrive, settle and fulfil the purpose for which they have been put on this earth.

And so, from that creation story onwards, it is not surprising that we find narratives of home cropping up regularly in the Bible. Abraham, in old age, becomes aware of a home that maybe he has hankered after his whole life, a hankering that becomes unbearable in his ageing heart, so much so that he and Sarah go off in search of it and, against the odds, they do find a homeland and a people. Moses becomes aware of an ache and a longing for home for his people that results in an eventual exodus from the foreign land of Egypt and a 40-year journey home. The prophets in Babylon minister to those who grieve deeply for the loss of their homeland, and they see a new vision of home that is not just fertile fields, flowing rivers and settled houses, but something much more than this that eventually takes shape as a world called the 'kingdom of God' by John the Baptist and Jesus. Important though a literal homeland is in the New Testament, we find a longing for home that is to do with justice, peace, fulfilment, freedom and, more than anything, love. The Gospels tell us the story of Jesus, a rabbi from Galilee who is different from all other rabbis, for he teaches about a homeland that is a place of true freedom from fear and shame. He is so committed to this home that he suffers unimaginable fears and shames to reach it for us.

Matthew and Luke tell us of Jesus' childhood home, which, by all accounts, is a safe and happy place. But we get a clue as to his real sense of belonging when he is baptised by John in the River Jordan. There, as he embarks on a journey from obscurity to a very prominent ministry, he breaks the surface of that baptismal water to a cry from heaven proclaiming him as 'my beloved son' (Mark 1:11). It is not fundamentally a house with walls, roof and furniture that makes a home; it is the sense of being safe because we are loved. Through his own mortal life that involved him having normal mortal needs, he demonstrated that the journey home begins with the knowledge of being beloved.

From her experience of working with the homeless, Sister Stan noted:

There are some people who have never known love. Such people have never been at home with themselves; they have never had the sense of being precious in God's hands; they have never realized that God has called them by name and loved them.[8]

The whole business of loving and being loved is such an enormous subject that it is hardly worth even trying to write something on it! Pretty well every song in the charts is about love and most films and books have a love story entwined in them somewhere. It doesn't take a psychologist to tell us that our sense of well-being is going to be shaped to some extent by whether we feel loved or not. Once we've acknowledged this, we cast our eyes across our world and see a very uneven distribution of love. Some people have lots of it and some have far too little. Some yearn for just one person to love them and treat them as special, because they have been lonely for too long; others have lost the one who loved them so dearly, and they spend hours of each day thinking back to the days when they took it for granted that there was a warm hand to reach out to in the dark. We could go to any country in the world and it would be the same—there are those who are fortunate to be beloved, and those who yearn to find love. And there are those who prefer not to have their fellow humans too close, and are quite at ease with being loved from a distance. We are all made differently, and so much in human relationships is about recognising and respecting this.

Beloved on the earth

From time to time there are very moving accounts of an 'unbeloved one' (to use one of John Betjeman's phrases) discovering a home-coming through encountering love. One story that has moved me is that of the American short-story writer and poet Raymond Carver. He was born in 1938 in Oregon. His father was a violent man, a sawmill worker from Arkansas who became dependent on alcohol, and his alcoholic fits of rage made Raymond's home anything but safe. At the age of 19 Raymond married a 16-year-old, and it wasn't long before he had three children to support. It became apparent that he was a talented writer, though some of his writing was deemed 'inappropriate' by polite society. Inside there was a deep struggle and, like his father before him, he found solace in alcohol. In the 1970s he was hospitalised three times for alcohol-related illnesses. Not surprisingly, his family left him and his wife eventually divorced him, and he was left very alone. However, with the help of Alcoholics Anonymous and great willpower, he heaved himself out of his addictive lifestyle and on 2 June 1977 he stopped drinking. He began what he called his 'second life'. The following year he met another writer, Tess Gallagher, and moved in with her. It was a wonderfully stable and loving relationship, and Tess's love for him undoubtedly contributed to his healing. He became the coordinator of a creative writing programme at Syracuse University and a professor of English. The house where he and Tess lived became so popular that from time to time they had to hang a sign outside that said 'Writers at work'. In 1988 he married Tess, but by now he was battling with lung cancer, and six weeks after the wedding he died at the age of 50. He was buried in Ocean View cemetery, Port Angeles, on the west coast of America.

Those who visit his grave today will find an inscription on his headstone, which is a poem entitled 'Late Fragment'. It reads:

And did you get what
you wanted from this life, even so?
I did.
And what did you want?
To call myself beloved, to feel myself
beloved on the earth.

As I read his words, I think of that wounded poet who came to the conclusion that the thing he had been searching for all his life was a place of belonging and safety on this earth, a place where he could, with all honesty, say he was beloved.

While our individual need for human love will vary depending on our life experiences, fundamental to all humans is a longing to be loved by God, in whose image we are made. If we follow the homing instinct for long enough it will lead us to a place where we find ourselves hankering to know whether, when all is said and done, our God in heaven who made us and put us in this world, for whatever purpose, actually likes what he has made. Like Adam and Eve in the garden, we wonder what he will make of us when he finds us. When he does, we are likely to default to either fear or shame and wish we could have some way of hiding. We sense we must have done something wrong, something that will bring about at best a divine sigh, at worst a fearful judgment. For many of us, an essential part of our healing journey has been the discovering of a

God who actually does love us, not for what we might become but for what we are now. Our homeland is the place where we know we are the beloved on the earth—beloved, that is, by our God.

I came across a story recently that beautifully illustrates this. In Frederick Buechner's *The Yellow Leaves* there is a chapter in which he looks round the room where he writes and comments on his various books and belongings that catch his attention. Among his pictures is one of Frank Griswold, who was for a time the head of the Anglican church in the USA. Buechner writes:

Frank Tracy Griswold, presiding bishop of the Episcopal Church, is smiling benignly in his dog collar and steel-rimmed glasses, that strikingly intelligent, articulate, sweet-tempered man. He told me that once when he was taking a shower, he distinctly heard a voice from somewhere saying, 'Why do you take your sins so much more seriously than I do?' His first reaction was to burst into laughter. His second was to burst into tears.[9]

There is something very touching about the scene: this American ecclesiastical VIP, no doubt exhausted from trying to hold together a church that is doing its level best to tear itself apart, enters one morning into his shower. There he is, not given to charismatic experiences such as hearing the audible voice of God, suddenly getting the audible voice of God. I imagine (if he is made of similar stuff to me) he might have expected to hear a message of concern about the state of the church. Instead it is a most personal message that is effectively saying, 'Frank, you berate yourself far more than I ever have done or ever will. Don't you understand? I love you.' And there, as the water pours over that burdened bishop like a baptismal stream, he cries like a child. There is a great vulnerability here, like Adam being caught naked in the garden. Yet Frank is not exiled from the garden. Far from it. He knows in this moment that he is the beloved on the earth. He is home and it is safe. All of us need those moments when we come to our senses and allow ourselves to dare to believe that we, too, are the beloved ones.

The swallow flies over the great Sahara desert thinking of one thing: a little shed in Derbyshire. With such intent she beats her wings with unflagging determination. She knows that if she can make it home, she will be able to bring about new life. The instinct in us is to search for paradise, that place where we can be fully ourselves without needing to be afraid and with nothing to be ashamed of. It is the place where we are sheltered by the knowledge and experience of being beloved by God. It is in the safety of that place that we will be able to venture into new life. In the next chapter I shall look a little more at how we can make this journey, and what can happen when we do.

For reflection

What was your childhood home like? Where were the places of safety for you in your childhood? What or who helps you to be who you really are today? What does the homing instinct mean to you?

Reuben's story (2)

For some reason my feet felt tired that afternoon. I looked down at them once or twice while he was speaking. There was his voice, the breeze nudging the branches of the fig tree causing the big leaves to sway, the stillness of the crowd, the flickering afternoon sunlight, and my feet planted firmly in the sandals lovingly made for me by old Simeon in his final days in this world. I could hear Ruth's voice now telling me that I should get some new sandals made. Yes, bits of them were falling off, but I didn't want to let go of this last gift from my old friend. These failing sandals still supported my strong feet. I looked at them, held by Simeon's leather and skills, and thought of all the journeys they had taken me on, helping me to meet good people like Simeon. But they had also taken me to places I should not have been to, places I could never tell Ruth about. For some reason it was those places that came into my mind as the Rabbi continued his story.

'The son gathered all he had, and he set out on a long journey to a far-off land.' I was looking at my feet when he said this. Instinctively my toes turned up, almost as if they were trying to catch my attention. What were they saying to me, these sturdy friends of mine? Were they saying, 'We know where you've been'? They had plenty of cause to accuse me with such remarks. But instead, I think they were saying rather sorrowfully, 'You have never allowed us to take you on a journey to a far-off land.' Poor old feet. It was as if they had been made for longer journeys, but all they ever got was a few miles here and there. Why had I lived such a safe life? Apart from those little mistakes, I had lived a very good life. People in the town admired me and looked up to me, because I knew and lived the law. 'Reuben and Ruth,' they would say, 'you can't get better than that.' But when I heard them say that, I felt ashamed and annoyed. Something in me didn't want them to admire this kind of life. It seemed so small. Even though, in this Rabbi's story, this terrible younger son had insulted his father so deeply and offended the Almighty so greatly, there was part of me that was envious of him. Imagine if I had all that money and was free to go to my far-off land. Where would I go? I had always longed to travel to Crete. I don't know why—I loved the thought of being on an island, by the seashore, the great sea, not just a lake. And they said the Cretan women were so beautiful... But there were also very bad stories about the Cretans. It was well known you should keep away from them. Of course I didn't want to go to Crete—what was I thinking?

The Rabbi went on with his story, telling us that this son squandered his father's money. It was easy to imagine. There were plenty of wild young men in a town like this who, given half a chance, would very easily get through large amounts of money on all kinds of ungodly pleasure. I found myself re-membering a time when I returned home after too much wine —it was the only time I had too much. It was not long before I married Ruth. I knocked the water jar over as I came in and fell to the ground, and, soaked in water, I laughed like a child until my father came over with his fury. He beat me so hard that I still had the bruises on my wedding day. I always believed he was right and I needed to learn the lesson. But somehow, now, on this afternoon, looking at my feet, listening to this story, something in me wanted to do something wild again. I wanted to get free, be ridiculous, spend money, drink too much wine, get into trouble. What was happening to me? They said this Rabbi had that effect on you. He had corrupted so many people, and now I felt he was seriously corrupting me. How did he do it? Was he using supernatural powers to get under my skin? I took my eyes off my feet and looked him hard in the eyes to see if I could see a clue as to the origin of this bad power. But I couldn't see anything bad. That was what disturbed me most. He was so clever, so devious that he was seducing even some good people like Nicodemus into respecting him.

As I looked hard at him, he turned his face and his eyes met mine. Although I had seen him once or twice in the region, it was always at a distance, and I was sure he had never seen me. When he looked at me now, though, I could have sworn he recognised me. I knew that if I were to go up to him right now, he would put a hand on my shoulder and say, 'Well, Reuben, how are you doing my old friend?' He was telling his story, but when his eyes met mine it felt as if everything in the world stopped. The wind stopped and the branches of the trees became still and the leaves stopped trembling; the crowd stopped shuffling, the dogs stopped barking and the donkeys stopped braying. Even the busy ants scurrying along the wall where he was sitting stopped their route march and held their breath and nodded their heads in anticipation. Surely the world had never been this still since it was created. And yet, in such stillness, what I wanted to do more than anything else was to shout 'Hallelujah!' at the top of my voice, and my feet were itching so hard that it took all my effort not to sprint off up the hill. I had never felt such powerful energy before. In those few moments I was planning my trip to Crete and I could see it all: the journey to the coast, the boarding of the ship, the heaving sea and billowing sails, and the arrival on the island with its great mountains rising up from the seashore. I was splashing in the sea and then climbing those mountains, right up to where the snow turned them white. I had never felt such a longing for adventure in my whole life. But he then looked away into someone else's eyes and, for me, the world started up again: the breeze blew, the leaves fluttered, the crowd shuffled, the dogs barked, the donkeys brayed and the ants busied themselves along the wall.

But the damage had been done in my heart. Somehow or other, that look he gave me, and the story of the son getting free of his father and going off on his life of adventure, triggered a longing in me that I knew could become like an enemy in my soul, something to battle with until my dying day. It was a new sin, as if I didn't have enough to contend with. I looked down at my feet again, and my toes were twitching up and down, rubbing against the frayed and worn edge of old Simeon's sandals. I could hear those feet saying, 'Go on, Reuben, you old stick-in-the-mud—get going on your adventure while you still have a chance.' I stamped on the ground to silence them, and several people turned round and stared at me for a moment, and one woman said 'Shush' very loudly.

The Rabbi heard the stamp of my feet, and he paused and looked up again straight at me. 'Then the famine came,' he said, and at that moment a cloud covered the bright afternoon sun and it felt as if we had suddenly entered a dark ravine. My toes stopped twitching and rested back in the old sandals. More than anything, I felt disappointed. Disgraceful as it may seem, I had been hoping that the son was going to have the adventure of his lifetime. But no, of course, life is not like that. It was inevitable. Good times never last. Now he would have to return to his angry father. Even as I stood there with my feet still as rocks, I felt the bruises of those violent fists endured all those years ago and, for a moment, I even felt the tears that poured from my drunken eyes when I escaped to the vineyard that terrible evening and lay in the earth among the rotting fruit that had been the cause of my sinfulness.

—— Chapter 2 ——

Working from home

The Romanian-born Jewish writer Elie Wiesel is one of the best-known survivors of the Holocaust. Based in the USA, he has been a most prolific writer. In the years following his terrible suffering, he has made admirable use of the experience for strength, wisdom and justice. One of his wise sayings that is often quoted is:

When you die and go to heaven and you meet God, God is not going to say to you, 'Why didn't you become a saint? Why didn't you discover the cure for cancer? Why didn't you change the world?' No, all God will ask you at that holy time is, 'Why didn't you become you?' Why didn't you become you?[10]

Quite how he came to that conviction I don't know, but at some point in his reflections on life and faith he came to this strong belief that what God is most interested in, as he inspects our lives, is whether or not we have become the person we were designed to be. I wonder whether Brother Ramon had this in mind when he looked at me with that piercing gaze and told me I had not yet become Michael Mitton. What I am discovering in these recent years of my life is a growing desire to become me, and yet also a recognition that discovering quite who I am is not an easy task. Many are the times that I have thought, 'Would the real Michael Mitton please stand up', hoping that, like they do in game shows, the real me would emerge and push past the imposters to the applause and delight of the crowd.

Around the time that Elie Wiesel was in Auschwitz, the Lutheran pastor Dietrich Bonhoeffer also found himself incarcerated. He was in Tegel military prison in Berlin, awaiting trial. With his usual mix of honesty, vulnerability and courage, he explored not only political and theological issues but also deeply personal ones. In his beautiful poem 'Who am I?',[11] he writes of his discovery that within him there are at least two characters: there is the one that most see, a confident, calm, cheerful man who bears misfortune 'equably, smilingly and proudly'; but there is another one that Bonhoeffer is also very familiar with: 'what I know of myself, restless and longing and sick, like a bird in a cage... faint and ready to say farewell to it all'. He wrestles with the question 'Who am I? This or the other?' Is he the calm, confident man full of faith or the 'woebegone weakling' who is angry and afraid? The poem ends with the simple yet profound conviction, 'Whoever I am, thou knowest O Lord, I am thine.' Bonhoeffer here gives us the foundation from which to explore: the knowledge that whoever we are, and whatever parts of us we discover along our way through life, we belong to God. We are entirely beloved of God. Once we know that, we know those parts of us that have yet to emerge from the crowd can do so with safety. Those other parts of us will not be judged, laughed at or scorned. They may be quite diffident, and a little pale from lack of daylight, but nonetheless they must come and be welcomed.

I know that I am now entering territory that is normally occupied by skilled psychiatrists and counsellors and without their skills there is a limit to how far I can go. But I have discovered there is a fair bit of exploration that can be done by that good combination of prayer, listening and common sense. With some careful listening we may well discover parts of ourselves that have wandered off like the prodigal son and need to be welcomed home. I write this with some conviction because such an experience happened to me, and it started with a dream.

The aelwyd dream

All of us have dreams, even if not all of us can remember them. In the world of dreams we do things we would never do in our normal waking lives. We calmly fly above houses and trees, meet famous people, and find ourselves walking naked down streets! We turn one way and we are in the events of the present, and another and we are back in our childhood. We weep and we laugh, sometimes even waking ourselves up with it. We meet people we have not seen for years, even some whom we have not thought of for years. We enter a world which is so different from our waking lives and yet one which is most definitely ours.

I can't remember when I first started to trust my dreams, but I know it was a long time ago. Dreams are shy creatures that usually rush away when we wake up. But occasionally, when we wake, we just glimpse a piece of the dream before it takes flight and dashes out of sight like the White Rabbit in Alice's Wonderland. Sometimes, however, with Alice's determination, we choose to race after that rabbit to get a better look at it and other bits of the dream come back to our conscious mind. At first glance our dream might be fairly unimpressive, and our conscious mind, the one that likes things clear, rational and acceptable, rolls its eyes and tells us there are more important things to be getting on with. But I've got more impatient with those rolling eyes, and increasingly I like to take hold of the dream and give it a fair hearing, because, as likely as not, it has something important to say to me. It is the bit of me that has come out under cover of dark, and speaks, albeit in its own language. Sometimes all that is happening is some sorting out of whatever is on my mind. But at other times it seems that this subterranean part of me is trying to catch the attention of my conscious mind, which is often the case for a recurring dream. It keeps banging on with a message until I get it.

It was six months before my sabbatical that I had a dream

which, far from fleeing when I woke, remained with me during the day as bold as brass, for it had something so important to say that it would not budge. There is nothing particularly remarkable about this dream and I simply record it here to illustrate how our dreams can hold important significance for us. As I tell my story, I hope it will help you to discover yours through the dreams that you manage to get hold of.

So here it is. The dream is located in Cumbria, in the rather grand setting of Rose Castle, near Carlisle, which at the time I had the dream was the home of Bishop Graham and Molly Dow. I have known Graham since he taught me at St John's College, Nottingham, in the 1970s, and I used to visit him at this great ancient house when he was Bishop of Carlisle. In the dream we are having a meeting in an upstairs room, but the roof looks flimsy because it is made of straw and is blowing off in the strong breeze. I suggest it might be safer if we go out into a nearby field for our meeting, and we do so and happily discover that someone has arranged some comfy old armchairs there. We settle down for our meeting, but I am having difficulty in hearing what people are saying. To make matters worse, it gets dark and I can no longer see the group. So I do the only sensible thing, which is to settle back in my very comfortable chair and enjoy the beauty of a wonderful early summer evening. I can see vividly the silhouette of the distant hills against the light of a rising moon. The world is so serene and in this serenity a number of trees fall gently to the ground. I watch them tumbling from the sky, upside down, with their roots flailing behind them. Suddenly it is morning and it is light. We walk back to the big house, and as we do so I become aware of a young woman walking on my left. It quickly dawns on me that this is a daughter whom I have never properly acknowledged. The full horror of this terrible omission hits me and I turn to her, struggling to find adequate words, and say, 'I'm so sorry, I've been a terrible father...', but before I can continue, with extraordinary grace and forgiveness, she lightly touches my arm and says, 'It's OK, Dad. I know, but I'm doing all right.' And there the dream ends.

Returning to Frederick Buechner once more, in *Now and Then: a Memoir of Vocation*, the second of his autobiographical books, he comments on dreams:

Part of what seems to happen in dreams—and what makes them some-times prophetic—is that in them you live out parts of yourself that have not yet entered your waking life either because you have never consciously recognized them or because for one reason or another you have chosen not to.[12]

As I woke from my dream, I knew this to be the case. I instinctively knew that the daughter in the dream was a part of myself that had not been properly acknowledged in my waking life. In this case, something in my subconscious self was saying, 'There is a bit of you that you have been ignoring for too long. It is time to acknowledge her.' My initial quest was to find out just what part of me was this unacknowledged daughter. This dream became the basis of my work with the counsellor on my sabbatical. With her skilful questions and insights she helped me find my meaning for this dream. In between visits I wrote new chapters of the dream, as she suggested, allowing my imagination, that close relative of dreams, to guide me as to what might have happened next in the story. In those three months I discovered much about myself through the dream and subsequent writing. I discovered that the daughter represented the creative part of me that I was not attending to sufficiently. I took up watercolour painting as a way of stretching those creativity muscles that were atrophied through lack of use.

However, there was a more significant implication for me, which emerged through exploring other aspects of the dream. The large house represented safety, security and to some extent the insti-tution of the church. But, for me, working for the institution was feeling dangerous—the roof was blowing off. The 'inside world' was dangerous. I needed to settle in the 'outside world', where I could be closer to creative life. And as for the trees, well, even they held significance. These were gifts from heaven to my earth. They were upside down because for me what was important was not 'getting to the top' but exploring the roots. It was the roots that I noticed, with their fascinating, spiralling dance as they fell to the earth. I knew I had to attend to my roots, and whatever work I got involved in would need to include a strong element of attending to nourishment, depth, renewal and all that gives strength to enable trees to grow. I have no doubt that I was dreaming of 'home'. That is, this night-time dream was designed to lead me to becoming who I truly am and to give me the confidence to be this person without rushing for cover because of fear or shame.

Of course, none of this happened without a fair bit of opposition, all of which came from within me. I identified a very active 'critical parent' voice (to use the language of transactional analysis[13]) which became very disapproving of the whole process. It is the same voice that mutters disapproving comments about my writing in this book. It tells me that no one is bothered about my dreams, and it is always trying to lead me into a more sensible life. But little by little this new daughter, the new 'member of my family', has become integrated in my life, and, as a result, I am more at home and I am becoming Michael Mitton. One practical consequence of this is that I realised that I had to move away from the safety and structure of paid employment, and I launched out into a new 'field', the freelance work in which I am now engaged. The dream is subjective—it is my experience. It is not exclaiming that the institution of the church is collapsing and that we must all dash out to whatever the nearby fields might be for safety. It is *my* dream, saying that, for *me*, working for the institution carries risk.

Rowland Evans has written a very thoughtful and poetic book called *My Sea is Wide*.[14] In an early chapter he writes of a conversation (imaginary, I think) with his mentor, a fellow Welshman called Dan. Rowland writes this book as he approaches the age of 70 and he is reflecting on what it means to dream at his age. In this case he is using 'dream' in the other sense of the word, which is to do with imagination, ambition and longing. But the two are related and meet at various points in the deeper parts of our lives. During their conversation Rowland and Dan exchange the following thoughts. Dan speaks first:

'You must find the courage to be as wild as your dream.'

'But as I reach for it, it is always just beyond me, and slips away.'

'Ah then, you have not yet met your dream; you have only seen it in the distance.'

'Then how do I meet my dream? Where does it wait for me?'

'Come now, bach, you have been this way before, many times. Dream needs its own space in you. It needs to find its home in you. No, more than its home, its aelwyd, the hearth of your home, the cradle of your belonging. Where the warmth of the glowing coals reaches the heart. The inner place where you come home to yourself; where you enjoy unconditional security; from where you will not want to wander… Let your aelwyd hearth become the place where you connect with who you really are.'[15]

It came as a delight to me to discover that another writer held the same conviction as I: that there is this inner place, this *aelwyd* where we can connect with who we really are. Our night-time dreams and our longing dreams are very familiar with this place and they will lead us to this place where we can come home to ourselves.

Vocation

When I became Director of Anglican Renewal Ministries (ARM) in 1989, one of my first tasks was to run a national conference for about 400 Anglican clergy and lay leaders. As a fairly young and inexperienced minister, this felt like a daunting task. The keynote speakers for my first conference included George Carey, who was then Bishop of Bath and Wells, and John Hughes, then Vicar of St Andrews, High Wycombe. The third speaker was Adrian Plass, whom I had not met before. He spoke at the first session and only arrived as I was saying some introductory words about him and wondering quite what I would do if he didn't turn up! What I noticed about this first conference was the way these three speakers all spoke most vulnerably: George described the pressures he experienced as a diocesan bishop, as well as his understanding of the pressures his clergy faced in his diocese; Adrian, with his typical humour, gave space for therapeutic laughter and tears and offered his extraordinarily perceptive and compassionate insights into our frail humanity; John, occasionally breaking down during his talks, shared of the huge pressures he faced in leading a large charismatic church through a time of great change and development, and yet, through his weakness, he gave such eloquent testimony of the grace and power of God at work. Each day ended with space for any who wanted to come forward and meet with someone who would listen to them and pray for God's healing and strength to touch them. It was here that I began to discover the huge range of pressures and hurts that pile on local clergy and leaders, and some of their stories were heart-rending. All through my years with ARM I never lost my admiration for the courageous men and women who would make their way to our conferences.

In latter years I have also worked closely with clergy from my home diocese, Derby, through leading a course called 'Developing Servant Leaders'. Again, I found myself working closely with church leaders facing a multitude of pressures, both from within and outside the church. What I have learned from all of this, as well as from observing what happens in my own soul as a church leader, is that the kinds of pressures that clergy and leaders have to face today seriously threaten our ability to find our way home. In effect they lead us into an inner exile. Gordon Mursell, at the beginning of his *Praying in Exile*, says that 'exile is any situation or experience in which you are not at home, and not in control of what is happening to you'.[16] If that is the case, many of our church leaders will feel themselves to be in some kind of exile.

The real problem with this is that if we are not effectively operating from our own inner homeland, we are very likely to be operating in a way that, from time to time, will come over as inauthentic. It will be apparent in our preaching, in our pastoral care, in our public ministry, that we are not being truly ourselves. I suspect the reason why some of us drift into operating from a state of inner exile is that in many ways it is simpler. We become what the church needs us to be, and there are fewer complaints and therefore less pressure. To tell the church what we are really feeling and reveal who we really are feels far too risky. Knowing the ease with which some criticise their leaders, such criticism aimed at the heart of who we are would be doubly wounding. No one likes having their home criticised by others. Nevertheless, despite these pressures, I have observed a number of leaders growing in determination to find their own inner homelands.

Some years ago the Bishop of Derby invited me to be the preacher at the Maundy Thursday service, an annual event where the clergy are invited to come and renew their priestly vows. It felt a daunting task to preach to such a congregation with all their experience and expertise. When the Dean greeted me on my arrival before the start of the service, he did little to reassure me by saying, 'This is most unusual, for it has always been either the dean or the bishop preaching at this service'! I climbed the pulpit steps as the Gospel procession ebbed back into the choir stalls, and I clung on to the pulpit to steady my nerves. In the end I preached too fast and, with a poor sound system in the cathedral at the time, few heard what I said, but I remember feeling particularly passionate about my message, and it was the first time I explored this theme of homeland in my preaching. As I looked across that sea of clergy, I said:

How do we know we are on a journey to home rather than away from home? Perhaps there are little signs: it's those moments when we feel we have come to our senses somehow; for a moment we take our eyes off our professional ministries and on to the Lord who has called us personally by name; when we find ourselves actually worshipping rather than leading a nicely polished act of worship; when we push through the absurd fullness of the in-tray and actually discover a little of what it means when people say we are human beings not human doings; when we experience the Spirit of God touching us and, despite our stuttering tongue and tired heart, we find ourselves preaching good news to the poor, and feel that anointing oil poured liberally down our weary soul, healing not only us but others through us.

In the years that followed that sermon, particularly through the leadership course I ran in the diocese, time and again I witnessed something of this actually happening and it has been one of the most rewarding things that I have experienced. In the last few years I have been in many small groups of clergy where they have risked a high degree of vulnerability in sharing personal stories of pain and struggle, and I have seen the wonderful compassion and care of their colleagues in response. This is a far cry from one of my first clergy chapter meetings in the diocese in the early 1990s. The Rural Dean asked for us to share 'more personally' (I think those were his words). One vicar present then said, 'Before we do, could we just check out what Lent courses we are doing in our churches?' That discussion took the full hour of the meeting, and the Rural Dean asked for a few moments of prayer together at the end. There was the usual moment of awkward silence, followed by one of the clergy present praying in a quiet and shaky voice, 'O Lord, it feels to me as if you have passed us by. Our roof is leaking, we cannot pay our share, and the congregation is dwindling. We have lost our way and lost our hope. Have mercy on us', and everyone mumbled an anxious 'Amen'. We then said the grace together and people rushed off to other important meetings. It took enormous courage for him to pray that prayer among his peers. In those days no one seemed to know quite how to respond, but I feel that, had he said that prayer in a chapter meeting today, there would have been a more supportive response, because I have seen signs that we have become better able to cope with each other's vulnerability. I like to think that the Developing Servant Leaders course has had some influence on this, as a core part of the course is the Action Learning Set in which a small group of clergy meet together with a facilitator and are committed to listening to one another in a disciplined way. Time and again I have found that this provides a safe place for honest sharing of our hopes and fears.

It is curious that, in thinking about 'home' and 'exile' in this way, it feels as if exile is the more secure place. It is the place where outwardly we can appear strong and competent as we cope with our circumstances. Home on the other hand can feel a very vulnerable place where we have to face our weaknesses honestly. But the point is that the vulnerability, the weakness, is there whether we acknowledge it or not. Exile is the place where we hide from it. Home is the place where we are willing to face it and, hopefully, where we can face it with trusted friends. Home is the place where the healing can begin.

As we discover our inner homeland, we can get a far clearer idea about our true vocation. If Bonhoeffer's question 'Who am I?' is one of the core questions of life, the next one is 'What am I here for?' Martin Luther King said, 'Set yourself earnestly to discover what you are made to do, and then give yourself passionately to the doing of it.' At the wedding of Prince William and Catherine Middleton in 2011, the Bishop of London began his address by quoting Catherine of Siena: 'Be who God meant you to be, and you will set the world on fire.' Only as we become who we truly are can we get on with what we have been designed to do in this life that has been entrusted to us. There is therefore a strong vocational dimension to this quest to find our inner homeland. Many are struggling in their work because they are not doing what they instinctively feel they have been designed to do. They sense an inner dissatisfaction. We can be nervous about exploring this, not least because we fear it might lead us to ending up out of work. But this understandable anxiety can rob us of discovering our true vocation.

The psychotherapist Fiona Gardner is author of *Journeying Home*, which has the subtitle 'Unlocking the door to spiritual recovery'. Like John O'Donohue, she sees a strong connection between homecoming and spirituality. Towards the end of her book she writes:

Journeying home starts with a glimpse of recognition that something needs to change. We are interrupted by a thought: 'Is this it?' 'Is this how it's always going to be?' 'I don't want to spend the rest of my life like this!' 'There has to be something more!' We wake to the realization that something needs to happen. Journeying home is awakening, a way of happening, and a relationship—with ourselves and with God.[17]

With her gifts as a psychotherapist she offers useful insights into how we can make that journey home. At heart, the journey is about a commitment to love ourselves as we are. How often have we heard preachers exhort us to do this; how often have we read books explaining why we have to do this; how often has a kindly friend told us that God loves us as we are so we must do the same. The fact is that loving ourselves is not as easy as they make it out to be! Nonetheless, although there are far too many things about me that irritate me to make this easy, I am committed to the journey. It's not about overlooking my faults and shortcomings and excusing bad behaviour and attitudes. It's certainly not about narcissism and going all gooey-eyed at myself in the mirror! Nor is it believing I am always right and everyone else is wrong. It is daring to journey to that place were I begin to see that I am a life that has been formed by the hand of God and that he made this life good, and he made it for a reason and he loved it into being.

It is to do with respecting the value of this life, recognising that it needs very careful stewarding and that given the right climate it can really flourish and produce much life for others. Love never ends up in a cul-de-sac—it always adventures out and multiplies. Loving ourselves in this kind of way inevitably leads to loving our neighbours.

During my sabbatical, apart from the weekly visits to my counsellor, exploring my dream of home, I visited about a dozen friends who have known me over the years of my life. I visited an old school friend who has known me since I was a child; I visited a friend who was at theological college with me; I visited people from parishes where I served, and from different parts of my career. Before I saw them I sent each a questionnaire, and the questionnaire was all about me! What gifts did they think I had? What did they sense had yet to come to life in me? What did they think I would be doing at this stage in my life? And so on. It seemed desperately introspective, but I really needed their help, their insight, their honest response to these questions. It was part of my way of finding an answer to Martin Luther King's 'Set yourself earnestly to discover what you are made to do.' I felt humbled by the care these friends took in completing the questionnaire. I met with each one and they went through their responses to my questions. Little by little a rather new and different shape of my vocation appeared.

All this, alongside my homing dream, led me to the conclusion that the way I was working had to change. The problem was that to change jobs would demand more risk and vulnerability than any previous job. For me, the journey home was not a journey to material safety and security. Quite the reverse! It has been a journey into far greater vulnerability, and yet there is absolutely no doubt in my mind and experience that at another level I feel more secure now than ever before. In my experience, the more I become who I was made to be, the closer I feel to the One who created me and called me to serve him in this world as me. Homecoming spirituality is all about discovering the presence of God in the midst of the person that is genuinely me. The more I have the courage to be myself, the more likely it is that I will know the love of God who yearns for me to come home.

I am very aware that my story is unique, just as every human story is unique. My homing story has led me to leave the security of paid employment and branch out into freelance work. For others it will be different, and there may be some for whom the process will be quite the reverse. The point is that all of us need to do something along the lines of this listening work with the help of good friends to discern the location of our true home. When it comes to our work, the question to ask is 'Am I working from home?' Some of us do literally work from home but this does not necessarily mean that we work from our inner home. Many church ministers work from vicarages or manses. They 'work from home', but those houses can sometimes actually drive them from their inner homeland as the houses can feel in some sense 'owned' by the parishioners or church members. In my last job for the diocese we lived in a diocesan house that had previously been a vicarage. My wife was quite surprised and disturbed when, a few weeks after we moved in, a couple of women arrived with large baskets and secateurs and asked if she minded them cutting some foliage from the bushes in the back garden as it was traditionally used for the church harvest festival. At that moment the house we lived in suddenly felt a little less like home. Of course this depends, to some extent, on personality. More extravert people might welcome such a visit and it may make the place feel more like home to them. But incidents like this illustrate that many church leaders can feel that the houses they live in are not exclusively theirs. I have been so grateful to my church employers over the years for providing us with lovely homes, but the home we now live in is actually our own home with no one else making a claim on it. For me, that makes it feel much more like home.

Whatever the work is to which God has called us, whether paid or voluntary, full-time or part-time, 'religious' or 'secular', we all need, from time to time, to step back and ask the fundamental question, 'Am I working from my inner home?' If not, we need to begin the kind of explorations I have been suggesting in this chapter to discover our pathway home.

For reflection

How do you feel about dreams? Have you had one that seemed to be especially important? Why not give some time to listening to what it might be saying to you?

Do you feel you are 'working from home'? What would you need to do to work in a way that is rooted in your inner home?

Reuben's story (3)

My sister, Judith, was four years older than me but she was only 17 when she had to leave home. After she left, neither my mother nor father would allow her name to be mentioned in the house. I remember the day well. I woke to the sound of someone washing by the well. I got up and saw it was Judith. I could tell something was very wrong and I went straight to her. She was frantically pouring water over herself as if she was trying to wash some dreadful stain away. 'Oh Reuben…' was all she could say. I had never seen anyone look so desperate. She hugged me so hard, pressing her soaking hair into my shoulder. After a few moments she suddenly became calm and she stepped back and looked me in the eye. She dropped her right hand to her belly and said calmly and simply, 'We will be all right. The Almighty will take care of us. You must not be concerned.' She picked up a bundle of things next to the well and without any more words she walked away, turning the corner of our neighbour's house, and that is the last I saw of her. Fifteen long years ago. My parents never spoke of her again. Her belongings were thrown out and it was as if she had died—only we were not allowed to grieve.

So, when that Rabbi talked about the wayward son in his far-off land, I thought of Judith, and a shiver went through me when he talked about the famine in that land. I could see her now, wherever she was, looking like a frail old lady, putting out a feeble hand to passers-by, begging for something to eat. I also imagined her child. I always imagined he was a boy. He would now be a little older than I was when Judith left home. I imagined the pain in his heart as he watched his mother begging. I imagined him living with the stigma of being born of unmarried parents. I imagined, I imagined, I imagined. This was my problem. Too much imagining. But I can't help myself—I imagine all too clearly. This is why the stories this Rabbi told disturbed me so—I could see them; I could smell them, touch them, feel them. It was not just my sister in that far-off land; I was there too.

I now listened intently to the Rabbi, who was telling us about this young man who spent all that money and was now having to feed the pigs. The shame of it! To be near such unclean animals is bad enough, but to be actually feeding them! I heard Shemaiah say, 'That's all the boy was good for', and realised that this was what the Rabbi must be getting at. To run away from home in this way and to disgrace your father can only lead to your downfall, and you can't get much lower than feeding pigs. I somehow imagined the Rabbi would be smiling at this point, as if to say, 'He got his just desserts', but the look on his face took me completely by surprise. He narrated this part of the story not as a natural consequence of sinfulness but as a terrible disaster that happened to one quite innocent. His face looked full of sorrow, as if he felt sympathy for the boy. I felt indignation rise in me, and I sighed loudly. Shemaiah had noticed this expression too, and he straightened himself up, folding his arms across his chest. He breathed in and nodded at me knowingly, as if to say, 'This is another of those subversive stories. Look out!'

It was then that I noticed a couple of women sitting on the ground just in front of the Rabbi. From the way they were dressed and how they arranged their hair, I was fairly convinced they were prostitutes. That was another thing about this Rabbi —he seemed to have an awful lot of prostitutes as friends. Of course you can guess what most of us made of that! Any decent man, let alone a rabbi, would kick them well out of his way to prevent any gossip. But this Rabbi actually seemed to invite them forward when he taught. How could he possibly condone what they did: the traps they laid for men, their terrible seductiveness for poor innocent men who have enough distractions from the path of holiness in their lives? After all it was one of these demons that had... on that dreadful day that Ruth must never hear about. The Almighty will never forgive me and so he shouldn't. But even more, he will never forgive such wicked women who trap innocent men. You should hear what my father has to say about such women.

I was just thinking about my father's opinion of these women when one of them started to cough loudly, though it wasn't really coughing. It was a kind of sobbing, yearning sound which she was trying hard to suppress. She was red-faced with embarrassment and covered her face as best she could. Her friend put an arm round her. There were a few jibes from the crowd around and lots of 'shhhh's. The Rabbi had been looking to the back of the crowd until this kerfuffle. Then, to my horror and amazement, he slipped off the wall where he'd been sitting and just lightly touched the shoulder of the woman in the kind of way a father would reassure his child who had just awakened from a nightmare. That little touch completely quietened her, as if a storm had suddenly been stilled. Then he was sitting back on the wall again. It all happened so quickly that I wondered if I had imagined it. Did he really touch this woman? Did he know how unclean this would make him? Did he realise what chitchat it would cause? Why did he seem so unconcerned about our perfectly good codes of decency and behaviour?

Despite wanting to look well away from them, my eyes settled again on the two women at the front, now snuggled together, looking up at the Rabbi. The afternoon sun had broken through a gap in the trees and shone brightly upon them both, a kind of very uncomfortable celestial beam of light. If the Almighty wanted to shine on anyone in that crowd it would not be them. But then I thought of Judith. Just suppose she had had to... well, sell herself in this way to provide for her child. Could it have happened to her? Surely not! She was far too good, such a happy, carefree soul. Yes, she was very beautiful; everyone said that. And she had been betrothed to Johanan, a very upright man, my father said; a very good match for Judith, for there was plenty of money in his family. That poor man was so upset, as you can imagine. Imagine, imagine, imagine. There I was again. I now imagined poor, beautiful Judith, somewhere in the north, maybe Sidon, if my mother's guess was right. I could see her leaving a little baby with some new-found friend, and then dressing herself like those women at the front of this crowd, with her hair down. Could that be her fate? Oh, surely not. But it could have happened. I could not be sure that it had not happened to her. And what of these two women? What was their story? Did they choose this life? Or had they too been hit by some tragedy which drastically changed their fortunes?

I could not believe I was starting to think like this. Up until now my values had been so straightforward. It was clear what was right and what was wrong. I knew who to trust and who not to trust. But something about this story and the way this Rabbi was telling it was getting well under my skin. I whispered to Shemaiah, 'I'd better be going.' But he didn't hear me—he was looking out into the distance and was biting his lower lip nervously. I know he had observed the scene with the two women and must also have disapproved. And yet as I looked at him his eyes betrayed a deep sorrowing in his soul, a sorrowing he did not want anyone to know about.

—— Chapter 3 ——

Home truths

In 2009 I was driving home from a meeting and there came on the radio a song by Paul McCartney called '(I Want to) Come Home'. He had composed it for the film *Everybody's Fine*. I was struck by the words of the song, which talk about how home is the place of home truths, the place where the truth of the matter is driven home. There is a sense that at home the truth stares you in the face and there is no avoiding it. And, to use McCartney's words, it is the place of remembering just who exactly we are. I like the idea of 'remembering', because that implies an instinct within us that has known the truth all along. We have forgotten it, and we have to remember it. It is the homing instinct.

Jesus once said, 'You will know the truth, and the truth will set you free' (John 8:32, NIV). Those who first heard this were offended, because such a statement, to their minds, implied that Jesus viewed them as slaves (v. 33), the ones who were not free. This saying of his comes in the context of a discussion with religious leaders and it continues, 'Jesus answered them, "Very truly, I tell you, everyone who commits sin is a slave to sin. The slave does not have a permanent place in the household; the son has a place there for ever. So if the Son makes you free, you will be free indeed"' (vv. 34–36). I am, of course, interested that Jesus refers to the 'household' here, which sounds to me very much like a home or perhaps, more strictly, members of the home. It is the slave who may look longingly at the household but could never feel fully part of it. The son, however, is fully at home and has a true sense of belonging. The Son's task, according to this passage, is to award us our freedom so that we can be fully at home in the household. Home is the place where the truth lies waiting, the truth that will set us free.

The two sons story

In Luke's Gospel this theme of home and freedom is developed beautifully in the parable to which I referred at the outset of the book. It could have many names: the parable of the two sons who thought they were slaves; the parable of the father who loved despite everything; the parable of the prodigal son; the parable of the house of grace; the parable of the journey home. It could be called by so many different names because it is so full of meaning. Certainly to call it 'The prodigal son' limits it far too much, not least because it completely ignores the role of the older brother. It is time to give some attention to this story because if any story is the definitive one for homecoming, this is it.

There are many books and studies on this parable, but I have particularly valued Kenneth Bailey's research in his book *Poet and Peasant*.[18] Luke 15 contains three 'lost and found' parables: the lost sheep (vv. 1–7), the lost coin (vv. 8–10) and the lost son (vv. 11–31). Bailey argues that all three of these parables have been very skilfully composed. Each has a home theme. In the first, the lost sheep is brought home (v. 6), resulting in a celebration in the home with friends and neighbours. The second takes place in the home, and when the woman finds the lost coin, home becomes again a place of celebration to which friends and neighbours are invited (v. 9). In this story, Jesus compares the celebrations in this home to the celebrations that go on in heaven when one person repents (v. 10). In the third story, the son comes home, and again there is a great celebration. One strong theme in each of these home parables is that of celebration.

For a clue to how beautifully crafted and constructed the third of the stories is, here is a little of Bailey's research.[19] He describes the parable as a parabolic ballad with twelve stanzas that match each other using inverted parallelism. All that means very little to me! However, when he lays it out like this, it becomes clear:

1 A son is lost—'Give me my share'
  2 Goods wasted in extravagant living
    3 Everything is lost—'he spent everything—he began to want'
      4 The great sin—'feeding pigs for Gentiles'
        5 Total rejection—'no one gave him anything'
          6 A change of mind—'he came to himself—I perish here'
          6' An initial repentance—'make me a servant (I will pay it back)'
        5' Total acceptance—'his father ran and kissed him'
      4' The great repentance—'I am no more worthy to be called your son'
    3' Everything gained—a robe, ring and shoes (restoration to sonship)
  2' Goods used in joyful celebration
1' A son is found—'My son was dead and is alive, was lost and is found.'

Bailey notes that this 'matchless ballad also has a type of counterpoint... The same twelve stanzas with their inversion seen above also relate to one another thematically using step parallelism.' This can be seen as follows:

The first six stanzas

speech 1
he leaves
in need but unrepentant

becomes a pig herder
eats nothing
is dying

The second six stanzas

speech 2
he returns
in need and truly repentant
becomes an honoured son
feeds on the fatted calf
is alive.[20]

Now, I'm aware that this may only be of interest to those who have done English literature A level. However it does show, among other things, that Jesus was a fine poet and constructor of stories. He clearly had thought long and hard about this story, and the fact that he constructed it so carefully tells us something about its value. He gave it to his disciples so it could be easily memorised and passed on from generation to generation. Its message was fundamental to his ministry and he was keen for his disciples to remember it and live by its truths.

This story begins at home and ends at home and involves a longing for home. David Adam, in his *Living in Two Kingdoms*, writes:

The shortest summary I have heard of this parable is:
   At home
   Sick of home
   Away from home
   Homesick
   Home.[21]

He suggests adding a final line for the older son: 'Not at home at home'.

The story begins with disturbance. This is not a settled family. It is a homestead where the younger child is restless. We don't know what age he is, but I imagine him being in his late teens. Is he restless because he looks at the life his older brother is leading and sees that it is not the kind of life that he wants to lead? Perhaps his life has already begun to fall into a dull routine: he gets up in the morning, and he and his brother go off with the hired hands to feed the cattle, mend fences, till the fields and manage the slaves. As time goes on he finds himself feeling 'there must be more to life than this'. Every now and again when he goes into town for a drink with his mates he comes across someone who has travelled to a far-off land and he starts to discern in his soul a longing for adventure. He wants to go to a far-off land too. He feels trapped, awkward in his childhood home. He's grown out of it. Interestingly, there is no sense in which Jesus is critical of his longing to adventure. When you get to the end of the story you get the feeling that Jesus has more of a problem with the stay-at-home son. It's right that children should want to travel, to adventure. In fact it says something very positive about this home that at least one of the children had a desire to explore the world beyond the borders of home. The problem was not the longing to adventure; the problem was how this younger son went about finding that adventure.

What he failed to appreciate at this stage of the story was that his was a home of grace. He assumed it was a home of law, probably because he had watched his brother working hard to keep the law. And this, of course, was one of the problems that Jesus was addressing. The tax-collectors and sinners, who were listening to this story with a sense of dawning hope, had swallowed the worldview given to them by the Pharisees: that the God of this world was a God of the law and the only way to remain in favour with God was to obey every law. How many in this world have looked at religious people and concluded that their God must be a cold, distant and judgmental God who demands allegiance through rigid law-keeping?

If the son had known his was a home of grace rather than law, he might have gone to the father and said, 'Dad, I want to see this amazing world. I'm ready to travel now—can you advise me how I can do it?' It is quite possible that the father of grace would have said, 'I will give you some of my earnings to go and explore. See if you can find ways to earn a bit of money on the journey. You know you can always come home if it doesn't work out. But go on, find yourself, discover this world.' But the younger son believed the worldview of his brother and assumed he lived in a home of law. He could not imagine anything different. What he did know was that travelling and living the kind of life he hankered after was going to cost money. I imagine him spending hours out in the fields thinking and scheming how he could get his freedom. The one thing that would make his dream possible was money, and the only way he could get this kind of money was to access the wealth currently locked up in his father's treasure chest that one day would come to him as his inheritance. The more he thought about it, the more he longed for this money as his key to freedom. Why should he wait? Thus one day he goes up to his father, presumably plucking up a fair bit of courage, and says, 'Give me the share of inheritance that belongs to me.' He cannot stand this home any longer—it feels like a prison to him.

Kenneth Bailey has done some research on what response this kind of request might have received in Middle-Eastern culture. He writes:

For over fifteen years I have been asking people of all walks of life from Morocco to India and from Turkey to the Sudan about the implications of a son's request for his inheritance while the father is still living. The answer is almost always emphatically the same... 'This request means— he wants his father to die.' [22]

The first audience of this story would have drawn a deep breath at this point, and they would have had a clear idea of how it should

66

continue. They would have expected the father to turn round angrily and say, 'Never! Now, for being so impertinent, you shan't have anything after I've gone. I am ashamed to call you my son because of what you have done.' But this father is different (it's a home of grace, not law), and the listeners would have been both amazed and shocked to hear that this father, unlike any fathers they knew, actually agreed to this request. How could he do so? It was unheard of to reward such disrespectful behaviour. But agree he does, because this father is more interested in relationship than laws or fortunes. We are told that he divided his wealth between his two sons (v. 12). Presumably the older son also got his share, which, according to Deuteronomy 21:17, would be double what the younger son got. But the older son has no interest in adventure, as far as we can see, and remains working the fields as a dutiful son.

So the younger son goes off to his far-off land, and it is an irony that going away from home he discovers the true quality of home. This parable that Jesus tells is, of course, designed to make us ask questions of ourselves and to evoke a sense of homesickness in us. In these opening verses there is a positive and a negative. The positive is that here is a child who longs to adventure. The negative is that here is a child who has got a false view of his home, and we, as followers of Jesus and children of God, need, from time to time, to check out how we are feeling about home.

Henri Nouwen, in his great work on this parable, *The Return of the Prodigal Son*, writes about the shocking nature of the younger son rejecting his home:

Leaving home is then much more than an historical event bound to time and place. It is a denial of the spiritual reality that I belong to God with every part of my being, that God holds me safe in an eternal embrace, that I am indeed carved in the palms of God's hands and hidden in their shadows. Leaving home means ignoring the truth that God has 'fashioned me in secret, moulded me in the depths of the earth and knitted me together in my mother's womb.' Leaving home is living as though I do not yet have a home and must look far and wide to find one.[23]

And he goes on to share his own story:

Yet over and over again, I have left home. I have fled the hands of blessing and run off to faraway places searching for love! This is the great tragedy of my life and the lives of so many I meet on my journey. Somehow I have become deaf to the voice that calls me the Beloved, have left the only place where I can hear that voice, and have gone off desperately hoping that I would find somewhere else what I could no longer find at home.[24]

When we feel restlessness growing in us, it is important to spend time with it, asking questions of it. The key question is 'Where am I?' Am I (as Henri Nouwen experienced) running away from home, fleeing the 'hands of blessing', because I have become deaf to the voice of the beloved? If this is the case, I need to rediscover the voice of the One who calls me 'beloved' in his home. Or have I lost my belief in the home of grace? Have I begun to doubt God's love for me? Have I started colluding with the Pharisee voices that keep telling me that it's all about law and I have failed once again? Or maybe I really am in a far-off land. I may feel I have been wandering for many years, perhaps all my life, in search of something, and yet the land I find myself in is a land of famine. Maybe my search might be that Raymond Carver yearning, to know myself 'beloved on the earth'.

So the younger son puts distance between his old home and his new world, hoping that this is the answer to his restlessness. But the problem is that he is not at home in himself. Rather than sitting down and really listening to the source of his restlessness, he does the most obvious thing—he expresses the restlessness by running off to a new life. But he can't leave his heart behind, and contained in his heart there is very likely to be a sense of being unloved, which, at one level, is extraordinary because we know his father is so loving. Yet it is plausible because the son has come to believe that his home is a home of law. The trouble for him now is, because he hasn't attended to his inner world and found home within, his contentedness is going to depend entirely on his outer world.

Driven by these unrecognised assumptions, the son 'squandered his property in dissolute living' (v. 13). The Greek for 'dissolute' is *asotos* and is not a common word in the Bible, but it appears in the Septuagint (Greek) translation of Proverbs 7, which is a word of warning about prostitutes. So possibly the older brother's assumption (v. 30) about how the younger son spent his fortune has some truth in it. If that's the case, there is a hint here that part of what this younger son was searching for was indeed love and affection, which of course he wasn't going to get from paid-for sex. It all amounts to a tragic story of waste and loss. The boy had won a fortune and lost it. And it wasn't his to lose—it was his father's hard-earned cash. Then the story develops: there is a famine. This far-off land that looked so promising, so full of wine, women and song, now has nothing to offer even if the son had money to pay for it. He stands there as a famished figure in a famine-stricken land. It is a picture of dreadful outer and inner emptiness. The place that once was to this young man a place of freedom has become a place of slavery. He knows he has reached a place of utter desperation when the pig food actually looks tempting.

The great moment of meeting

Finally there is a turning point. It comes in verse 17, which is often translated as 'he came to his senses', but the Greek literally means 'he came to himself'. Kenneth Bailey has pointed out that this is the centre point of the ballad, the verse around which the whole story turns. This is the key to the whole story. So what exactly does it mean? How on earth do we 'come to ourselves'? What kind of internal integration does this imply? I think, for me, it was my dream that gave me a clue about this. In my dream that my subconscious self situated in that beautiful field in Cumbria, I discovered part of myself that I had ignored for too long. I pictured this part of myself as a daughter. After working on this for some time with my counsellor, I read again verse 17 with new insight. Yes, I had very clearly 'come to myself', in the sense that I had made a move towards a part of myself from which I had been estranged. In a way, the dream made it easy for me, and I appreciate that for others such a journey can be arduous. Fundamentally, however, coming to myself begins with listening to myself.

It will be clear by now that, on my own journey of exploration, the writer and minister Frederick Buechner has become something of a mentor and guide for me. I once found on the Internet a short filmed interview of him in which he was asked to identify his core message, if he had one. He answered very quickly and openly that it was to do with listening. In *Now and Then: a Memoir of Vocation*, he writes about the value of listening to his life even when it is at its most mundane:

Taking your children to school and kissing your wife goodbye. Eating lunch with a friend. Trying to do a decent day's work. Hearing the rain patter against the window. There is no event so commonplace but that God is present within it, always hiddenly, always leaving you room to recognize him or not recognize him... Listen to your life. See it for the fathomless mystery that it is. In the boredom and pain of it no less than in the excitement and gladness: touch, taste, smell your way to the holy and hidden heart of it because in the last analysis all moments are key moments, and life itself is grace.[25]

From my work with Acorn's Christian Listeners, I learned the great value of listening, but I think it is only relatively recently that I have really been learning to listen to my own life. It is about a discipline of noticing the things that move me and asking why they do. I now want to know why I love the fact that, outside my study window, the trees I look on move me. Why is it that when I visit the National Gallery in London and look at the 17th-century artist Claude's huge painting of the marriage of Isaac and Rebecca I am filled with such a sense of wistful longing? Why do I love Mark Knoplfer's 'Brothers in Arms', even though I have never been on a battlefield? Buechner lays great store by noticing lumps in the throat and moisture in the eye. We can all too easily dismiss them as silly nonsense, assuming there are far more important matters to be getting on with. But they may be clues to what is happening in my inner world. I 'listen' to the beauty of the trees outside my study window, and I feel praise rising up in me to their Creator; I 'listen' to Claude's painting and the quality of light in the far-off hills, and I hear something about hope and my need to find points of hope in this world; I listen to Knopfler's 'Brothers in Arms', and I hear my need for secure friendships in a world of many pressures.

Another way of detecting how this journey of 'coming to myself' works is by listening carefully to films and stories that move us. For example, there is a film called *Enchanted April*, based on the novel by Elizabeth von Arnim, that has become one of my favourites. It is essentially a very simple story, but one which focuses on a group of people who all 'come to themselves'. Lottie and Rose, two married women living in post-First World War London, share the misery of empty relationships with their spouses and decide to rent an Italian castle for the spring to get away. In order to pay the rent, they advertise for two other women to join them. They are joined by the initially very fierce Mrs Fisher, an elderly widow who knew many famous authors in her youth and is now struggling with a lonely and regimented existence. The other companion is Lady Caroline Dester, a celebrated aristocrat who is sick of the false life her fame has brought her and longs for a time of blessed anonymity.

These four unlikely companions make their way to San Salvatore, a seaside Italian castle drenched in wisteria and sunshine. It is not long before they are joined by Lottie and Rose's husbands, as well as the owner of the villa, George Briggs, who lost much of his sight in the war. As the film progresses, the enchantment of San Salvatore starts to have its effect on the characters as they discover pieces of themselves that have been dormant for a long time. The character that perhaps moves me most in this film is the initially cold and very formal Mrs Fisher, played brilliantly by Joan Plowright. Once or twice we are allowed to hear her thoughts as she asks, 'What's happening to me?' for something is most definitely happening. Much to her surprise, she allows the tender and creative parts of her to emerge, which have been trapped inside her for too many years, and a sign of this is that she begins to paint the flowers that flourish so freely in the garden. Little by little she loses her dependency on her smart and polished walking stick, which, at the end of the film, she plants in the ground and leaves there. Earlier in the film they heard the legend of a man who had planted his walking stick in the soil of San Salvatore and, because the land was so blessed, the stick sprouted leaves. The film ends with a close-up of Mrs Fisher's walking stick, which, sure enough, has also sprouted leaves. For all of the characters in this story there has been a springtime, a thawing in the soul, an embracing of more vulnerable parts of themselves and daring to share them with others. It is a true homecoming story.

The younger son in our parable, then, has encountered a part of himself that he hasn't properly met before. He has had to travel to a far-off land and squander his father's wealth in order to find one thing: himself. He has now 'come to his senses': he is listening to his senses—that normal, God-blessed instinct for seeing things as they really are. As he kicks the pig food to one side, he reflects on the fact that even the hired hands, those who have no real connection with the family, have all the sustenance they need, and more to spare (v. 17), whereas he is starving to death. The home that he was so keen to escape from had something he had never really seen before, something that had been staring him in the face but which he couldn't recognise. It was that in that home there was generosity. Whether you were the oldest son or a distant hired hand, you always had enough and more. While he believes that his father cannot welcome him back as a son, he hopes that he might be able to return as a hired hand, so that he will at least have the physical nourishment he needs.

As the son considers his journey home, he sees it very much in terms of returning to a person rather than a place. 'I will... go back to my *father*' (v. 18, NIV). He set out to explore a world, but he is now returning to meet a person. Even so, he still hasn't had his Raymond Carver moment yet; he assumes that he will never be the beloved on the earth, especially not the earth of his own homestead, after what he has done. He still assumes that the home to which he now returns is a home of law not grace, and so he is expecting something like a court martial. He thinks he'll survive, because he is fully contrite—he has his speech prepared. Heaven and father will forgive him—that much he is reasonably assured of—but in a law-world the relationship cannot be repaired. The best he can hope for is being a hired hand, but that will be OK.

Many of us hearing this story for the first time would probably have felt much the same. We would nurse a kind of wild hope that the father would not be too cross and that there would be somewhere in that homestead where the son could lodge. The Pharisees would still be hoping for a more severe outcome. They would be hoping for a thorough lambasting of the good-for-nothing boy, for the terrible insults issued to his father. The tax-collectors and sinners would be fearing that the story would turn out this way as well, returning them to the old world where there were few winners and many losers. I suspect not a single person was prepared for what happened next in the story.

But while he was still far off, his father saw him and was filled with compassion; he ran and put his arms around him and kissed him. Then the son said to him, 'Father, I have sinned against heaven and before you; I am no longer worthy to be called your son.' But the father said to his slaves, 'Quickly, bring out a robe—the best one—and put it on him; put

*a ring on his finger and sandals on his feet. And get the fatted calf and
kill it, and let us eat and celebrate; for this son of mine was dead and is
alive again; he was lost and is found!' And they began to celebrate.* (vv.
20–24)

If ever there was a line in scripture that for me sums up the heart of
the gospel it is the first line of this passage. We are left in no doubt
about what it is that motivates this father. It is compassion. In a
law-based world, there is not a lot of value given to compassion.
In a grace-based world it is what makes the world go round. The
Greek word for being compassionate (*splanchnizomai*) includes
the word *splanchna*, which is a term for the guts. In Rembrandt's
famous painting of this story, you get a clear sense of this as you
see the welcoming hands of the father pulling the shaved head
of his famished and exhausted son to his stomach, his guts, the
place where compassion is felt. It is extraordinary that Jesus should
declare through this story that a driving force for God's dealings
with his humans is compassion. For the Pharisees this is far too
fluid, far too emotional. It makes for an insecure world where you
don't really know where you stand, where people could get away
with anything. And yet, says Jesus, this is what you will find in
the heart of God. Our English word 'compassion' is also full of
significance—it means literally to 'suffer with'. The father, therefore,
rather than looking on dispassionately at his wayward son, allows
himself to get inside this son's life and feel what it is like. In his
heart, he has gone on this journey with him. He has not condoned
his bad behaviour or tried to excuse it, but he has taken the trouble
to listen deeply to his son, to make an attempt to get to know the
self that the son has come to in verse 17.

I love the sense of movement and travelling you get in this
story, not just from the son but also from the father. Significantly,
the only person who is static is the older son. When the father
first sees the younger son, he is a long way off. There is something
wonderfully comforting about the fact that even when we are

a long way off, the Father is looking on us with compassion. Whether it is due to what the Bible calls 'sin', or whether it is pressure, or tiredness or our mood—whatever the cause—much in this world can put distance between us and our God, and when this happens we worry that we will somehow escape his notice, even his love and care. But this story shows clearly just how long-sighted the Father is. The moment the father sees that the son is making his way home, he runs towards him. Remember, this parable tells us something about the nature of God's love and compassion, and it is wonderful that we have this image here, which you don't get very often in scripture, of a God who runs. The scene brings to mind those rather hackneyed old films where two lovers are for a time separated but are then reunited, and they fling whatever baggage or jackets they might be holding to one side and run towards each other until they meet with hugging, kissing and laughter. It is exactly this kind of delight that we get in this story, which again would have been embarrassing to the Pharisees, who would have been more comfortable with a more dignified image of God.

For the son, this dramatic and energetic welcome must have felt quite extraordinary. He sees himself as a hired hand, but the father sees him as the son who has come back from the grave. When did the son first see the father? As he came over the brow of the hill and saw the home that he had left so triumphantly all those months ago, did he expect to find his father waiting by the gate? Did he dare to imagine that his father had been thinking about him every waking hour of each day? How well did he even know his father? I think the answer is 'hardly at all', whereas the father seems to have known so much about the son. As I think about my own discovery of God as the one who knows me, even when I am far off, it brings to mind Psalm 139, that poem that speaks so eloquently of the knowledge God has of each of us. Perhaps the son might have written his own version that would have included verses like this:

Where can I go from your spirit?
Or where can I flee from your presence?
Even if I journey to a far-off land and spend all my inheritance on wine,
women and song, you are there.
If I give my life to feeding unclean pigs in a land of famine, you are there.
If I finally come to myself, you are there also.
You have been there all along.
Even in the dark corners of my heart where I hide my shame and guilt,
you are there because my heart is not dark to you.
Where I prepare my little speeches to try to put things right,
Even there you are, your arms stretched out to embrace me.

And so the father and son are reconciled and at long last the son realises that this place that he once ran away from is a more wonderful home than he could ever have imagined. A law-based home could only go so far: 'Break the rules and you end up a hired hand.' In a grace-based home, the rules are quite different. Compassion rules—a healing compassion that changes lives. So if you are to embark on a journey inward to explore your own homeland, you will need to go with grace-filled compassion, knowing that your Father in heaven knows your far-off lands so well, and even if there are patches of darkness, they don't put him off.

The older son

The story, as we know, doesn't finish with the celebration, although the first hearers probably assumed that this was the end. I suspect there was an irritated Pharisee who was about to raise his authoritative hand and say, 'With respect, a point of order...', when Jesus said, 'Meanwhile the older son...', and suddenly the Pharisees and all that is pharisaic in all of us are in the spotlight. As is so often the case in Jesus' parables, we can feel an affinity with the person who at first sight appears to have been treated unfairly.

At face value, it does seem rather unfair that this son, who has worked so hard and faithfully for so long and has not squandered his father's money, is not celebrated in the way that the younger son is.

Some years ago I went to a musical in Swansea based on the remarkable life and ministry of Evan Roberts, who became an extraordinary preacher in the Welsh revival at the beginning of the 20th century. The musical was written by Mal Pope, and I particularly loved the way he had fashioned the characters to be both exceptional and holy people yet also very vulnerable, with some of the human weaknesses we recognise so well in ourselves. I was particularly moved by one song that was sung by a man who played a contemporary clergyman who had been quite critical of Evan Roberts' ministry. While Roberts drew thousands to his meet-ings and saw God do extraordinary things among the people, there were other ministers who had faithfully preached the gospel and cared for their flocks diligently over many years without ever seeing anything like that kind of revival. Thus, Mal puts into the mouth of one of these ministers a heart-rending song called 'You never threw a party for me', and as I watched the character on stage perform, I realised his was a song I'd heard from so many hearts over the years expressing that desperate sense that we have worked so hard for God but apparently achieved very little, whereas others seem to reap the rewards of ministry so easily.

It is, I think, this kind of thing which gives us some sympathy for the older son. And yet, if we stop at sympathy, we'll miss the point. It is the way with Jesus' parables that we must pay particular attention to the moments we feel indignant or offended by them and wonder why they disturb us so. In this story, although the older son seems to be presenting a reasonable objection, at the heart of the problem is his comment in verse 29, 'all these years I have been working like a slave for you, and I have never disobeyed', revealing all too clearly his misconception that the house is a house of law. It is significant that he does not go direct to the father but goes to a slave to ask what is going on, which suggests that he is more at ease with a dutiful slave than with a compassionate father. From his perspective the celebration is quite unjust and he distances himself from his brother by referring to him as 'this son of yours' (v. 30). It is arguable that the father has been as much on the look-out for the older son's return as the younger one's, but the older son keeps stubbornly refusing to enter this home of grace. Instead, he remains a critical bystander, jealous of the celebrations.

In my own journey of 'coming to myself', I have discovered quite a strong resistance from a 'critical older brother' voice in me. I have noticed that I am not alone in this as so many labour under this kind of critical voice. I sense that this must be something not only to do with our own personal histories but endemic in our culture also. Ask any group to embark on a piece of creative work such as writing poetry or drawing or painting, and nearly always there is a rush of apologies for the standard of the work, as if there is a stern figure in the corner of the room ready to criticise anything that looks poor.

I became particularly aware of this critical voice during one of the vocational interviews on my sabbatical that I mentioned earlier. I went to see John Hughes, who at the time lived in Birmingham. I had sent him my questionnaire, and he had given it much thought in preparation for our meeting. As soon as our discussion moved from the usual happy banter of catching up on news to the questionnaire and my vocation, John leaned forward and, looking at me over his half-moon spectacles, he said, 'Michael, the main thing I want to say to you is that you are a poet. You have a gift with words, and you must use it.' His main conviction was that I had to give more time to writing and speaking. I immediately became aware of two strongly conflicting feelings in me: the first was of delight, that someone I respected so much should affirm a particular gift in me; the second and the stronger feeling, however, was one of anxiety in the face of a barrage of imaginary critical voices that strongly disagreed with John. They were saying things like 'You are certainly no poet. We can think of at least a dozen friends of yours who are far more gifted with words than you are.' There was also a rather more sinister and crafty voice which said things like 'You know, John is really trying to affirm you here to boost your confidence. You know he's exaggerating a bit to help you. You know the struggle you have to find words, and you are right to feel pretty insecure about this, because the fact is, old friend, you really aren't too impressive.' And so they would go on.

I am fairly sure that I am not alone in this kind of experience that produces such disabling self-doubt. What are we to do about such inner voices? Of course, some criticism can be helpful and can help to improve the quality of what we offer, but for many of us the voices can be more damaging than helpful. The parable is a useful guide, however. The father takes the initiative of going out to the older son, rather than simply ignoring him. The critical voice felt unable to join in the party, preferring to pronounce from a distance. But it cannot be allowed to remain at a distance—we have to go and meet it. And I have found that, having identified this critical voice within me, I am much less submissive to it, and much more prepared to go out to it and confront it. Most of us have these troubling critical older brother voices that all too easily pronounce with apparent authority from a distance. It can be very releasing to meet them head on. Sometimes we will need to carefully listen to the voice to find out where it is really coming from. At other times, when the voice has succeeded in disempowering us, we may need to draw from our strength and give it a good talking to. Either way, confronting rather than avoiding is the way modelled for us in the parable.

I have only been able to touch lightly on this wonderful parable, but I hope it is becoming clear that this most skilful of tales told to us by Jesus provides a wonderful map for the homecoming journey. All kinds of things may have happened in our life experience to make us feel we are in a far-off land, but we are never out of reach of the compassionate gaze of the father who yearns for our homecoming.

The journey home begins with us 'coming to ourselves', that preparedness to listen to what is going on inside ourselves and to know that, whatever it is, it is not beyond the reach of the Father in heaven who calls us beloved on this earth. Many of us may feel a strong resistance from the older brother whose mindset is that of law rather than grace, and whose critical voice is particularly hard on all within us that wants to be free, creative and truly ourselves. But the Father goes out to that voice too and pleads with it to let go of its critical ways and join the party. The older brother in us, therefore, needs also to come home.

For reflection

What parts of you do you feel are more hidden? What might have kept them hidden? Are there critical inner voices, like that of the older brother in the story, that have threatened them?

You may like to read the story again (Luke 15:11–32), asking God to speak to you afresh through it.

Reuben's story (4)

The mention of the starving boy made me feel a bit hungry and I started to look forward to the meal that Ruth would be preparing for us. The Rabbi said the boy was even thinking about eating some of the pig food. I have been hungry before, but never that desperate! I still felt no sympathy for this lad, given how he had treated his father. It was his own silly fault; he got himself into this mess, and he'd have to get himself out of it. So I was interested to see how the story would develop. The next words that the Rabbi used were so simple yet they seemed so stark, so sharp that I felt I had been prodded by one of those spears the Roman soldiers delight in using on us. He simply said about this boy, 'he came to himself'. The words were as simple as that. They were not particularly profound, and yet they were puzzling. At first I assumed he meant the boy became sensible at last and decided to make a responsible decision. But the way the Rabbi said 'he came to himself' made it sound as if he had rounded a corner and discovered the most wonderful scene, too beautiful, mysterious and difficult to describe. Those few words fired my imagination again: what if I rounded a corner and found I had arrived at myself? What would I look like? How might I find myself?

I thought of the scene—I knew exactly where it would be, by the big rock at the path that runs along Shemuel's vineyard from where there is that spectacular view across the valley. I'd turn round the corner, and there I would be. I pictured myself standing there, as if waiting to be found, and I realised that I did not like what I saw. I saw on my face such disturbance and perhaps, more than anything else, fear. What could I possibly be afraid of? The scriptures tell us quite clearly that if we fear the Almighty there is nothing we need be afraid of. But the fear was there, whether it should or shouldn't be, and I looked at it fair and square. Time now seemed to be suspended and I was given a chance to watch the drama happening on the stage of my own soul. And so I looked at myself and I saw the restless eyes.

'Why such fear?' I asked him.

'That night,' he said, so quietly I hardly heard him.

I knew straight away what he was referring to. It was the last night that my sister, Judith, was with us. I remember the suppertime. She was looking so beautiful but also anxious. Johanan, her betrothed, had been at the sabbath meal with us, but he had been restless throughout the meal, eating little. I did not see it at the time, but as I thought about it now, I realised what it was that made him so uncomfortable. It was guilt. He left earlier than usual, and I went off to my bed, leaving the others talking around the table. I went off to sleep until I was awoken by the terrible sounds of my father shouting and my mother and sister weeping and pleading. Judith was crying out things like 'He forced me', and my father was calling her terrible names like 'temptress'. Again and again he talked about shame coming upon the family. I had no idea what they were talking about—nothing made sense. I longed to speak to them, but cold fear pinned me to my bed and all I could do was desperately pray for it to end, which it suddenly did with my father leaving the house and slamming the door behind him. I heard little else after that, for my mother and sister spoke in whispers. It was the next day she left, she and the life within her.

I shivered as I finally acknowledged what actually happened in my family that night. For years I had believed my sister was a 'temptress', leading the innocent Johanan into her bed. But I now heard that word 'forced', screamed out by my desperate sister, and I heard my father again and again accusing her. How could it be that he did not believe his own daughter? Why was he so obsessed about the family being shamed? This 'self' that I was meeting on this country road was willing to admit to things that I had refused to hear. It had been easier and safer for me to believe my father's story, for to challenge him would lead to further beatings. This self I was meeting knew the truth but it simply left him alone and afraid. How could this self ever look his father in the eye again?

'He came to himself,' said the Rabbi. The young man came to himself on that hillside with pigs snuffling at his heels and his belly aching and a thousand regrets in his heart. 'He came to himself.' I think the Rabbi repeated it, or was it just echoing around in my head? I looked up and for the second time he was looking straight at me. He knew. I was in no doubt that he knew exactly what had happened in my home all those years ago. He knew I had been limping through life ever since, yet never realising that I was. Somehow, by some disturbing alchemy, he had seen into my soul. It was not I who had come to myself but he who had got there first. It was as if I had rounded the corner in my imagination and there he was, in conversation with the haunted man that was me. As I say, all this happened in the space of a few moments, but I experienced it as if time slowed to a crawl to allow me to catch every part of it. And we looked at each other. He and I had arrived at myself. There we were, a little group in the road, wondering what to do next.

I then heard his words, which were the last words I wanted to hear: 'He said to himself, I will get up and go to my father...' I would sooner descend to Sheol itself than return to my father, for how could I face him now? He turned his own daughter out of our house so that he would not have to face the shame of having a bastard grandson in the home. And he had drawn me into the lie, and I had acquiesced. Because of my fear of him, I had not listened to the truth. The Rabbi was still looking at me and I heard his voice again, like an echo in a deep chamber of my soul, and the words I heard this time were 'You can say to yourself, I will go to *my* father', and I realised that he was urging me to take a quite different journey: to go to the Almighty, the one this Rabbi insisted on calling 'Abba', much to our annoyance. I saw myself on the road, listening to this invitation. But I sensed dark and shadowy figures around me, with their arms crossed and frowns on their faces, disapproving of this chummy language for the Almighty. I heard my father's cynical and dismissive words about this 'Galilean upstart of a rabbi'. I watched my frightened self look up and, raising a hand to hush all those competing voices, I distinctly heard myself say, 'I want to come.' And I knew also that no power on earth could now stop me. I was on my way to a Father who had known me from the foundations of the earth but whom I had only glimpsed from afar. Quite how he would greet me, or what he would think of me, I did not really know. All I did know was that I wanted to go to meet him, even if in the end it would destroy me to do so. I just had to find out who he was, and there was no turning back.

—— Chapter 4 ——

Seeking a homeland

I cannot imagine what it must be like to be an exile. Many people in different parts of the world would envy me living in my homeland, for they have been forced to live in exile for social, political or religious reasons. Occasionally I have met refugees and asylumseekers. I have spoken to a young pastor from the Congo, and heard something of his pain at leaving the land where he grew up and of his sense of dislocation and his search to find a new land where he can settle. I have talked to a young woman from Eritrea and listened to her sorrow at being separated from her family. I listen as best I can and feel appalled at the tragedy that has befallen them. I also note their extraordinary courage and resilience in the face of what, for me, is thankfully unimaginable.

In her book *Far from Home*, Clare Nonhebel shares stories of people who are homeless and those who have become refugees. She writes:

The word 'home' must be one of the most emotive in any language. Everybody has an idea of home—an idea that has little to do with four walls and a roof, and more to do with a feeling of being at one with the world and having a place in it. For some, the word conjures up an image of coziness and security; for others, a nightmare. For emigrants and refugees, it is a bundle of remains of memories clutched desperately to their minds as they travel further and further away from the reality of home, which may never be seen again—or which may no longer exist.[26]

She writes movingly about her encounters with the homeless and refugees and how they found ways of making sense of their dislocation, in some cases so much so that they have effectively become tutors to all of us who are searching for home:

It may seem that… we too may be far from home. We may even be far behind them on the road home, for they have faced their homelessness and survived it, whereas we have not been so forcibly confronted with our own rootlessness and aloneness.[27]

In the Bible we have one major story of exile, experienced by the people of God in 587BC, when the armies of Nebuchadnezzar broke through the high walls of fortified Jerusalem and ransacked the temple and the king's palace and pulled down those great buildings, and proceeded to raze every fortified town in Judea to the ground. Many of the survivors of this devastation were taken on a 500-mile route march through the desert to live in a refugee camp outside the great city of Babylon. We get an insight into the emotional trauma of these people through such scriptures as Psalm 137, which begins with the lament:

By the rivers of Babylon—
there we sat down and there we wept
when we remembered Zion.
On the willows there
we hung up our harps.

The psalm ends with the terrible vindictive wish that the babies of their tormentors will be killed (v. 9). However, this beleaguered and desperate group of exiles were not left comfortless, because prophets emerged who carried to the people powerful words of the Lord that brought them hope and healing.

In 1986 the American Old Testament scholar Walter Brueggemann published a book called *Hopeful Imagination*.[28] As far as I know, he was one of the first to draw comparisons between the crisis experienced by the people of faith in the exile of the sixth century BC and the crisis experienced in today's church. Though the contexts were entirely different, both communities experienced a rapid collapse of a culture that had survived for a thousand years. For the sixth-century Israelites, it was the end of the era of habitation in the promised land, which latterly depended on the succession of kings who lived in Jerusalem and directed the people to worship in the great temple. For late 20th-century Christians in the West, it was the collapse of Christendom that pushed church culture and beliefs right into the margins. Given that it had been the forming influence of the culture of much of the northern hemisphere for so long, the experience for Christian people has been traumatic. However, Brueggemann argues in this book and in a succession of other works that the writings in the scriptures from this exile period provide a rich resource for the church to enable it to flourish as it too has to journey through a time of huge cultural upheaval. Thus, according to Brueggemann, the message delivered by the prophets and poets of the exile becomes very relevant to us, and part of that message is a calling to come home:

The poet in exile sings his people to homecoming. And that is a theme to which the exiled church in America is now summoned. The gospel is that we may go home. Home is not here in the consumer militarism of a dominant value system. Home is also not in heaven, as though we may escape. Home, rather, is God's kingdom of love and justice and peace and freedom that waits for us. The news is we are invited home (cf. Luke 15:17).[29]

We are now well settled into the 21st century and the 'exile' to which Brueggemann refers. Most people who are under 40 years of age have very little idea of what the world of Christendom was like, but the middle-aged and older are likely to hold memories of it: a place where school assemblies usually had Christian prayers and hymns, and most children became familiar with the basics of the Christian faith; a land that respected the Sabbath such that very few shops were open on that day, and few sports were played and test matches held a rest day. Most people venturing into church would recognise some of what was going on, even if they weren't personally convinced by the message. When Billy Graham made his last visit to Britain in the mid-1980s it was in the very last days of Christendom, so when he stood up and said, 'The Bible says…', there were still a good number of unchurched people around who were sufficiently influenced by Christendom to know that the Bible had some authority. Nowadays, however, if a prominent evangelist were to say, 'The Bible says…', most would respond by saying, 'So what?' Christian beliefs, values and customs are very much seen as an option among many others. Today's society has often been described as a 'pick and mix' culture, with many people following a mixed bag of beliefs, drawing bits from Christianity, astrology, Eastern religions and whatever the latest celebrity might be recommending. I remember asking one bride-to-be why she wanted to be married in church, and she replied, 'I like the karma I get in your church', and it never occurred to her that there was any contradiction in what she was saying. In some ways I was quite encouraged that she did feel a sense of peace in the church. As it is a 'pick and mix' culture, some bits of Christendom have been picked and are surviving, such as attendance at Christmas services and church weddings, but vast swathes of general knowledge about the faith have been lost.

For many older church members these are deeply disturbing times. They, their parents and grandparents lived in a world where it was relatively easy to get their bearings, despite the advances and changes of industrial society. Church remained solid in the middle of it all, and you could go to church and sit in the same pew, sing the same hymns led by the same organ and listen to the same collects and liturgies that previous generations enjoyed. Furthermore, even those neighbours who didn't come to church generally had some respect for Christian beliefs and values. Much of that has collapsed, however, in a relatively short period of time.

Today the neighbours know little or nothing of the faith, and inside the church it can seem even more strange. The place that once felt so much like home can now feel nothing like it. This is particularly so for those who love traditional worship—when modern clergy come along in brightly coloured clerical shirts, installing digital projectors, giving film-clip sermons and replacing the organ with light rock music groups, it can feel immensely disturbing. The more modernisations there are, the more the sense of exile and the greater the loss of a sense of home.

Of course, what may be happening in this kind of scenario is that the minister is trying to create a home for the unchurched, who may never find a sense of belonging in a traditional church culture that feels quite alien to them. For those who have little or no experience of corporate singing and little delight in sitting on a hard, cold seat for an hour or more, are not used to listening to a lecture method of communication, and have little understanding of liturgical words and customs, church can feel anything but home-like. Ministers are therefore torn between trying to meet the needs of some of the members and trying to make church feel something like home for visitors. This is one of the factors that can make leading a church so stressful nowadays!

Lessons from the past for our future

To get our bearings on this, let's do what Brueggemann suggests: go back to the ancient texts first delivered to a very disorientated people and see how they can help us today. Let's go back to that riverside scene in Babylon, where the exiles are lamenting that they can't sing the Lord's song in a foreign land, and they are filled with thoughts of anger and grief and loss (Psalm 137). Some time ago I visited an exhibition on ancient Babylon in the British Museum and realised that I had never appreciated just how grand a city Babylon was. It was far more glorious than Jerusalem, far more sophisticated and far wealthier. This would have made it even harder for those exiles who once believed that their city was the greatest and their temple the finest in all the world. The size and grandeur of Babylon caused the most uncomfortable questioning, just as the sheer power of our secular and materialist world can make our faith-world appear very vulnerable at times.

Displayed in this exhibition was the beautiful oil painting *By the Waters of Babylon*, a famous depiction of Psalm 137 by the Pre-Raphaelite artist Evelyn De Morgan. In this work painted in 1883, we see a collection of mostly young people gathered disconsolately by the waterside, and scattered among them are the lyres that no longer have any use or meaning for them. Some of the figures are bent over with grief, and some are just slumped in despair. Some are attempting to comfort each other. In the centre is a young woman who is kneeling with her hands clenched tightly together as people do in yearning prayer. Her head is slightly lifted as she gazes in the direction of a grey-bearded man who looks as slumped and depressed as any of them. He seems rather isolated in this group of young people and his cloak looks dark and heavy compared with the brighter colours and thinner materials worn by the others.

At first, when I studied this figure, I felt a sense of overwhelming loss. Then, whether it was wishful thinking or some kind of insight into the artist's intentions, I sensed movement in this old man. I saw him not as a man given up to despair, but as one who had inhaled every part of the suffering of his people—and his heavy cloak spoke of the stifling air of that grief—but had now caught a quite different scent on the breeze. Something was dawning on him, just as the light in the picture suggested a rising sun. Quite who this old man was supposed to be I don't know. All I do know is that as I looked hard at that picture in that low-lit exhibition, with the muffled sounds of visitors slowly shuffling their way past the various exhibits, I saw this old man as the prophet. I imagined him heaving himself to his feet, in his heavy dark-blue robe, and with twinkling eyes and with a voice louder and deeper than the waters by which his people were slumped, I heard him cry out, 'Comfort, O comfort my people, says your God.'[30]

I saw the young woman at the centre drop her hands and look up in expectation; I saw the slumped figures wipe their hands over their damp faces and blink as if someone had turned a bright light on them. I saw those in the background move forward to hear his message. I saw the sun shimmer its way above the horizon. I saw the old prophet shake off his years and his grief as he rose to his feet and his ever-strengthening voice declared, 'Speak tenderly to Jerusalem and say to her, "All is not lost. Far from it!" A voice cries out, "In the wilderness prepare the way of the Lord, make straight in the desert a highway for our God." You may feel that this place where you find yourself is a parched and barren place, but watch out! God is building a highway down which he is coming in power. So say to those devastated cities of Judah, "Here is your God!" and he's coming with extraordinary strength and also with gentleness. For who else has measured the waters in the hollow of his hand and marked off the heavens with a span? Judeas and Babylonias come and go, but our God goes on for ever.'

This passage of scripture that I have paraphrased is Isaiah chapter 40 in our Bibles and it must have been utterly transforming for those first listeners who had the ears to hear and were willing to step out of their grief and understandable self-pity. The message to us is similar to the one they received, and it is essentially 'Get a perspective on all this. Christendoms come and go like those ancient kingdoms did, but the nations are just a drop in the bucket, and cultural eras are dust in the scales, and all the idols, the pop idols, the screen idols and sports idols, the banking idols, the advertising because-you're-worth-it idols, the ecclesiastical idols —well, they are all ridiculous. Have you not known? Have you not heard? Has it not been told you from the beginning? Have you not understood from the foundations of the earth? It is God who sits above the circle of the earth. The Lord is the everlasting God, the Creator of the ends of the earth. Grasp this, and you won't be weary. Quite the reverse—you'll rise up with wings as of eagles.'

We need to get this into our liturgies and worship: we need words to express our laments and hurts, but also we need this sense of the extraordinary grandness of God that transcends the powers of this world. Once we have done this, we can begin to get a sense of the location of our true home.

The kingdom of God as home

In his book *Cadences of Home*, Brueggemann writes:

The preacher's theme for exiles is homecoming. The home promised to exiles, however, is not any nostalgic return to yesteryear, for that home is irreversibly gone. Rather the home for which the exiles yearn and toward which they hope is the 'kingdom of God', an arena into which God's good intention is decisive... It is no stretch to link homecoming to gospel to kingdom. The linkage is already made in Isaiah 40—55 and in Ezekiel 37:1–14... Consider then what it means to be exiles, awaiting and hoping for homecoming to the kingdom of God! In the Bible, the image of 'Kingdom of God' is stitched together by narratives of miracle and wonder, whereby God does concrete acts of transformation that the world judges to be impossible. The 'Kingdom' is a time and place and context in which God's 'impossibilities' for life, joy and wholeness are all made possible and available. [31]

What I see happening to those exiles in Babylon is that they were being offered a radically alternative vision of home. Home was not simply returning to their old land and rebuilding the walls, houses and temple, important though that vision was to the people. The prophet Isaiah was clearly directing them to a different homeland destination, one that involved a mysterious 'Suffering Servant' who is referred to several times. The extraordinary poetry of Isaiah 40 to 55 features this servant who will suffer for the home-comers as he inaugurates a new age. El Shaddai (Almighty God) will place his Spirit on him (Isaiah 42:1) and, with an unexpected combination of power and humility, he will demonstrate what home really can be in this world and give us glimpses of what an eternal home might look like. Retrospectively we understand this servant as a reference to Jesus, who ushered in the kingdom of God.

I need to return for a moment to my mentor, Buechner, because he has written a whole book on home with the appropriate title, *The Longing for Home*. In the first chapter he tells us about a preacher called George Buttrick who made a great impact on him when he was a young man. He writes of how Buttrick, when he was preaching on a Sunday before Christmas, 'peered out at all those people listening to him in that large, dim sanctuary and asked... "Are you going home for Christmas?"—and asked it in some sort of way that brought tears to my eyes and made it almost unnecessary for him to move on to his answer to the question, which was that home, finally, is the manger in Bethlehem, the place where at midnight even the oxen kneel.'[32] He ends that chapter by saying:

I cannot claim that I have found the home I long for every day of my life, not by a long shot, but I believe that in my heart I have found, and have maybe always known, the way that leads to it. I believe that Buttrick was right and that the home we long for and belong to is finally where Christ is. I believe that home is Christ's kingdom, which exists both within us and among us as we wend our prodigal ways through the world in search of it.[33]

If it is the case that in all humans there is this powerful homing instinct, a longing for home, a longing for a place where we can have a true sense of belonging, where we can be fully who we are without fear or shame, where we know we are the beloved on the earth, where we can become all that we are meant to be in life, then it is vital we find that home. More and more I find I am drawn to the obvious yet wonderful discovery that the home we all long for is none other than the kingdom of God. This kingdom is the place where we can be fully ourselves without fear or shame, where we can fulfil our potential and where we can be at peace. To return to the parable of the two sons, the kingdom of God is the home of grace, at whose gate there is a Father who waits with bated breath for any who are returning from their far-off lands.

This, then, is the powerful gospel message to everyone who travels through our world that is full of both delight and tragedy. Interestingly, if we take Brueggemann's point, this kingdom, this homeland, is one full of wonder and miracle and 'impossibilities'. In other words, what we long for is a home that is more than the normal run of things. How else do we explain so many children's fascination with magic and mystery? How do we explain our delight in fantasy stories and films? How do we explain the delight so many feel in the Narnia, Lord of the Rings and Harry Potter stories? It is all part of this longing for home and our instinctive belief that ours is a world where we can be surprised by miracles, despite everything.

I believe John the Baptist caught on to something of this as he too linked Isaiah's prophetic message of home with the kingdom of God. He is the voice in the wilderness predicted by Isaiah (Luke 3:4) and, in that chapter of Luke describing John's message and ministry, he declares that the coming Messiah will baptise with the Holy Spirit and with fire. John is calling out to a people who have been in spiritual exile for too long. Their hearts are desperately dry and they are bereft of the fire of God that purges the world of injustices and wrongs and is a blaze of light in a darkened world. So John calls out, 'It is time'—it is 'high time'. John is baptising people in Bethany (John 1:28), which we are told is 'on the other side of the Jordan' (NIV). The Jordan was deeply significant in the minds of the Jewish people. It reminded them of Joshua's final march to the promised land—the end of the wilderness wanderings and the entering of the homeland where they would truly belong. The people in exile in Babylon also longed to return across the desert and cross the Jordan and be back in the homeland promised to them. John is, in one sense, ministering to a people who are on the wrong side of the river, in exile, and he is setting them on the road home, a road which passes through the baptismal waters. Baptism is about letting go of the old and becoming open to the new. By offering baptism, John is saying, 'Come on, let go of your exiled life that is burdened by shortcomings and failings. Cross the Jordan and come home to where you truly belong.'

This became a journey that Jesus demonstrated through his own baptism, and the process is full of significance for us. As he emerges from the water, the Holy Spirit comes upon him in fulfilment of Isaiah 42:1, and the voice from heaven proclaims him as the Father's beloved son. Yes, there is no doubt that he is the beloved on the earth by the Father in heaven. The coming of the Spirit in this story is connected with the voice of love, and it always is—and the homeland that Isaiah spoke of to those weary exiles was one that would be full of the Holy Spirit: 'For I will pour water on the thirsty land, and streams on the dry ground; I will pour out my Spirit on your offspring, and my blessing on your descendants' (Isaiah 44:3, NIV).

John makes very clear that Jesus is 'the one who baptises with the Holy Spirit' (John 1:33), so the homeland of the kingdom is this Spirit-drenched place. Years after this event, the apostle Paul was reflecting on the life of the Spirit in that brilliant eighth chapter of his letter to the Romans, and he too observed the strong link between the gift of the Spirit and the sense of being the beloved on the earth:

For all who are led by the Spirit of God are children of God. For you did not receive a spirit of slavery to fall back into fear, but you have received a spirit of adoption. When we cry, 'Abba! Father!' it is that very Spirit bearing witness with our spirit that we are children of God. (Romans 8:14–16)

This, of course, brings us back to the story of the two sons. The younger son discovered what true sonship meant for him, whereas the older son betrayed his view of home when he told his father, 'all these years I've been *slaving* for you' (Luke 15:29, NIV). We could say that the younger son was led by the Spirit to the point where he could call his father 'Abba', whereas the older son remained closed to the Spirit in his mindset of slavery.

A brief look at these scriptures therefore reveals a message about home that is a message for all humankind. As mentioned earlier in the chapter, even regular church members may feel exiled in our post-Christendom society and need to find their way to a rediscovery of the kingdom. Those who love the way they remember church being 40 or 50 years ago and still long for its return can be like the slumped figures by the waters of Babylon, who are hoping that one day they can pack up their bags and return to Jerusalem, back to the good old days. Just like the Babylonian exiles, however, such people need to move forward and discover a homeland that is not 'home as it used to be' but a place that is the Spirit-blessed life of the kingdom. Indeed that is the quest for all of us, whatever our starting point. Finding it may well involve letting go of 'former things' in all kinds of ways. But in such letting go we open ourselves to entering our true home, where we can receive anew the gift of the Spirit, enabling us to experience to our very core the knowledge that we are daughters and sons of a God who has infinite compassion and love for us.

The curious thing is that this discovery of the kingdom of God as home does not mean that we then feel less at ease in this world. In my experience it is quite the opposite. The more I discover a true sense of homeland in the kingdom of God, the more I love this world. I see so many meeting points between this place that I inhabit and the 'unseen' world of the kingdom of God. I am discovering that this beautiful, though damaged, world is full of messages about the kingdom world. After all, many of Jesus' parables used images from this world to explain the meaning of the kingdom of God. David Adam, in his book *Living in Two Kingdoms*, helps us to see how we can actually be at home in both 'kingdoms'—the kingdom of this world and the kingdom of God. He writes:

When we are at home in both kingdoms, we are able to delight in the world and be at home with God. We acknowledge that we are created beings but that we are able to act as co-creators with God. The living in two kingdoms is a life-extending venture and a joy of knowing that the two are one in God. [34]

Inis Moir

One of the many gifts that the rediscovery of Celtic Christian spirituality has given to us is this acknowledgement that so many of the things of this good world can speak to us of the things of the kingdom of God if only we have the ears to hear. Many people have explored places of importance in Celtic history to learn more of this.

I decided to end my sabbatical by taking a trip with my good friend Russ Parker to the Aran Islands, which lie off the west coast of County Galway in the Republic of Ireland. On a cool and blustery day Russ and I met at Luton Airport and flew to Galway Airport. After a welcome Guinness and Irish stew in Galway, we took the taxi up to the little airport at Connemara. In that taxi we fell into conversation with an elderly man who had lived all his life on Inis Moir. He told us of his travels to far-off countries and then, wiping the mist off the inside of the taxi window, he looked out across the sea to the island that was his home and said, 'I live on the island and I have travelled the world.' He had clearly spent time visiting other countries, but something about the way he said this suggested that the one inevitably meant the other. Living on that breezy little island gave him a longing to explore the world. A true home is the base point for adventure. He was living in the spirit of the Celtic monks who occupied those treasured pieces of land 1500 years before him.

A small six-seater plane bumped us over to Inis Moir, the middle of the three Aran Islands, and we made our way to our little hotel. We were given a warm welcome by the owner and an enthusiastic one by his dog, who was clearly part of the family. The dog's name was Guinness, and sure enough his body was black and his head white! There is something vulnerable about living on a small island—you know that you are much more at the mercy of the elements than normal. The onset of stormy weather could keep us there for several days, and no sophisticated planes or ships could help us. And yet, despite this vulnerability, I also had a curious feeling of homecoming, which I have known in other places I have visited that are steeped in Celtic history. In the case of these islands, the history was to do with Breacon and Enda, two great Irish saints of old who inhabited the islands along with their evangelistic bands who lived, worshipped and studied together, before venturing off to share the gospel that burned in their hearts. They lived on the island and they also travelled the world.

The following morning greeted us with a beautiful November sunrise, and I have seldom known such a sense of inner peace. I found myself trying to put into words my experience. They assembled themselves like this:

When the world wakes beautiful
And the great Artist
Magnifies his message in a crimson sky
And the calm dark waters enfold us
With a tranquillity from our future,
It is then that my tepid fears slip from me
Leaving my soul warm to the touch.

Any anxiety I might have had about being on a remote island, far from my normal dwelling place, slipped from me and I was free to adventure. After a hearty Irish breakfast, we took a long walk to the north of the island, where we found the remains of an eighth-century collection of church buildings known as the 'Seven Churches'. This was the site of Breacon's original community. Among the various broken-down walls, ancient gravestones and apparently random heaps of stones was a small square area defined by a low wall with a little broken cross against one of the walls. The locally written guidebook informed us that this square area was called 'The Bed of the Holy Spirit'. We were so intrigued by this that we knew we could not just look at it but had to experience it, and rather gingerly we stepped in as you do when putting a toe into a swimming pool to test the temperature of the water. In this case the 'water' was very inviting, and we both found it to be a place that seemed to be charged by the Spirit, such that prayer flowed freely and all kinds of prophetic insights filled our minds. It was a truly blessed moment.

As we reflected on this during the long walk back, we grew to love this notion of a Bed of the Holy Spirit. If you think about the house where you live, your bed is probably the place where you feel most secure. It is where you retreat to for rest and the renewal of sleep. Sleep, of course, is the context for dreams, and I thought about that well-known passage from the prophet Joel, who spoke about how the Spirit would come and enable us to dream (Joel 2:28). The Bed of the Spirit is the place of resting in the Spirit, of renewal, and also of dreaming and seeing things that we don't normally see. For me, with my sabbatical shaped very much around the exploration of a night-time dream, this held special significance. But the experience also encouraged me to reflect on our local churches. Like Breacon of old, could we not expect our churches to be places where people can discover a 'Bed of the Holy Spirit', that part of the home where we can rest, be renewed, find healing and dream the dreams of the Spirit?

If the kingdom of God is the homeland for which all humans instinctively long, we need to explore how churches can be Spirit-filled places where people, whether of mature or infant faith, long-standing members or seekers, can come home and find rest and renewal and can begin to dream their dreams. We shall explore this further in the next chapter.

For reflection

How do you find living in today's 'post-Christendom' society? What do you think you might have to let go of in order to find your way home? What difference does it make to think of the kingdom of God as your home? If you are part of a church, how could it have a 'Bed of the Holy Spirit' in its life?

Reuben's story (5)

How long the Rabbi had been talking in that dappled afternoon light I don't know, but I felt I had been standing in the shade of that tree for most of my life. So much had passed through my mind and heart, and yet I think he had only spoken a few words. In a matter of a few moments, he had taken me to meet myself, and what I had found was a man with a shocking secret and the disclosing of that secret left a terrible wound. As he continued with the story, I felt such an ache for Judith; I had such a yearning to see her again. I had foolishly conceded to my father's wicked command that we view her as dead and never even mention her name. I hated to think of the pain that must have been in her heart. Even now I started planning to find her—surely my mother would have some inkling of where she was. I would insist she told me, and I would go the next day. Judith must know that at least one of her family still loved and trusted her. She had always been such a strong person that I was sure she would not have been overcome by all that had happened. She was a survivor and I had seen not only hurt in her eyes that day she left us but courage and determination too.

The Rabbi's voice broke into my thoughts and I heard the words, 'Father, I have sinned against heaven and against you and am no longer worthy to be called your son.' The very mention of 'father' now sent a dart of fear into me, and I could feel my heart beating faster. I sensed both fear and rage within me as I thought of my own father—his drinking, his rages, the beatings, but worst of all what he did to Judith. It was he who should be returning to me begging for forgiveness. But in the midst of my indignation I heard the Rabbi's voice and looked at him again. He had got up from the wall and was standing, waving his arms around in excitement. I heard the words 'filled with compassion... ran to greet him... threw his arms around him and kissed him'. I could not believe my ears. What was he trying to suggest? That the disgraceful way this son had behaved did not matter? How could all that go unpunished? What kind of a world was he trying to present to us? One with no justice at all? I looked at Shemaiah, who was frowning and shifting impatiently from foot to foot as if he wanted to walk away. I felt sick in my stomach—I couldn't accept a world where all this wickedness would go unpunished.

I decided to walk away before I blurted out something I would regret, and was just about to tell Shemaiah when I saw the two women in the front row, the ones I was sure were prostitutes. They were beside themselves with grief—it was embarrassing to watch them. They, of all people, should be punished. But then seeing them reminded me of my most terrible sin, the one I could tell no one about, that dreadful time... I knew the Almighty could never forgive me for that great transgression, and he would surely never forgive those women, wailing and weeping in the dust. The Rabbi paused in his story, and then bending down to them he took the hand of one of them—can you imagine the disgrace of this! He took her hand, and as he did so he continued his story. I see it now so clearly—he, stooping down, kneeling in the dust in front of these two red- and wet-faced sinful women. I saw the way he held the woman's hand—she laid it in his palm, and he gently stroked the top of it is with his thumb and, with the broadest smile on his face, went on, 'But the father said to his servants, "Quick, bring the best robe and put it on him. Put a ring on his finger and sandals on his feet. Bring the prize calf and kill it. Let's have a feast and celebrate! For this son of mine was dead and is alive again; he was lost and is found."' As he said those words, 'lost and is found', he looked at both women and then to my horror looked up at me and, using the same smile as he had used for those women, he repeated the words 'he was lost and is found'. As he stood up to continue the story, the two women became as still as a sail in a sudden calm. The whole place was so quiet, I hardly dared to breathe. In those moments, in a way that at first filled me with horror and shame, he seemed to put me and those two women in the same class. But that's where I belonged—I had no doubt about it. I was no better than they, and he knew it.

Guilt is like a steel helmet. You feel the weight of it, and it means you can't move freely; you can't see much and you can't hear much. All you feel is its grip on you. I had always felt it that way until that moment. But that look from him somehow unbuckled that helmet and I knew at last I was free—I could breathe freely again. I knew for certain that the Almighty had forgiven me my sin. Others might not be able to forgive me, and I might still find it hard to forgive myself, but I knew in that moment a condemned man had become a freed man. I had been dead and now was alive. I looked down at those women, people I had once despised, ones I had viewed as the cause of my downfall, and I now knew the only instinct within me towards them was to help them. I would even have touched their hands myself had I been near enough to do so.

To say I was shocked by this would be the greatest under-statement! I, a most respected Pharisee, thinking this way! I then thought of my father: dark thoughts still filled my mind when I thought of him, but something got me to look beyond my own disgust and hurt to wonder why he did what he did. What far-off land had he wandered to that he had become such a distant man? What had hurt him so? I could never excuse what he had done, but in those moments I realised that the God that this Rabbi was presenting to us was so vastly forgiving and generous in his love that he would throw a party even if my sinful father should make his way to him. Could that be possible? What about all the people who had lived good lives? They were the ones who should get the celebration first.

I assumed the Rabbi had finished his story when he got to the bit about the party, but there was more to come, and the final part of his story broke down the last bit of defence I had. It would have undone me completely had there not been someone in the crowd who came forward at the end of the Rabbi's story to touch me on the shoulder and bring more healing to my soul than I could ever have imagined.

—— Chapter 5 ——

Open home

One Sunday morning, a young couple came to St Paul's Church, where I serve as Priest-in-Charge, to enquire about having their wedding in the church. They came to one of our morning Communion services, and afterwards I spoke with them and gave them the usual information about weddings at St Paul's, together with the application form, and they went off and made their plans. They came back the following week with their completed form. This time, it was not our Communion service but our 'Soul Breakfast', a completely different kind of event that takes place in our church hall. Some months later I was talking to this young bride-to-be and I asked her how it was for her, as someone in her 20s and completely unfamiliar with church life, coming to St Paul's for the first time. She answered, 'When I came for the first time, I stopped outside the church and felt so nervous that I thought I was going to be physically sick. But when we came the next week to Soul Breakfast, we immediately felt at home.'

That conversation has lodged uncomfortably in my soul as I have a strong suspicion that she was not alone in feeling very anxious when approaching the threshold of a church for the first time. What causes this anxiety? What is it about church that seems so intimidating? When I ask people about this, they can seldom explain it, but the overriding concern seems to be about entering a building where sets of beliefs and codes of behaviour are likely to be at odds with the culture with which the person is familiar. I have sat through many seminars and talks where national figures are published to do with church attendance, and one of the statistical facts that always emerges starkly is the significant increase in the number of people who have never darkened the door of a church in their life-time, not even to attend a wedding or funeral. Therefore, for millions of people, what happens inside the church building on a Sunday morning is a complete mystery. I would guess that for most their assumption would be that inside that building is a group of mostly older, out-of-touch people who practise beliefs and customs that belong to a bygone age. Further, they may assume that if they were ever to enter the church building, that group of people would do their level best to indoctrinate the visitors with their beliefs and customs. Not surprisingly, few want to take that risk, for one of the features of today's culture is a strong resistance to being told what to do and how to think.

My leadership of St Paul's is a voluntary role, as I earn my living in other ways, so I only have a limited amount of time to give to the church. This means I have to work as part of a team of volunteers, each of whom is carving time out of a busy schedule to help a little local church grow and be all that God needs it to be. One of the things we discerned early on in my time at St Paul's was that God wanted us to be a church that made its life as accessible as possible to visitors, especially those who had little or no experience of church. This is how we got started on a series of café-style events and services with the word 'Soul' attached to them. Originally these were evening events (Soul Café and Soul Space), but at the time of writing they are all-age morning events (Soul Breakfast and Soul Sanctuary). We have always run these alongside more usual ways of doing church and in this regard we are, to use Archbishop Rowan's phrase, a true 'mixed economy' and see real value in both. What I notice, however, is that the Soul services, by their very nature, are instinctively more welcoming to the person who is not familiar with normal church culture. One person told me that what he loves about coming to Soul Breakfast is that he feels allowed to be himself. He once had a strong faith, but it was severely tested through a family tragedy, and the church of which he was part was unable to help him face his questions about God. However, there is something about Soul Breakfast, he said, which makes it feel quite safe to bring his questions, and he feels he does not have to live up to anyone's expectations. I hear in that something of the homing instinct, the longing for a place where we can be ourselves without fear or shame.

We really chanced upon the concept of Soul Breakfast, having found it very difficult to make provision for the few children who came to our normal services. We decided instead to craft an event to appeal specifically, but not exclusively, to families. We are still working on it, and who knows where it will go. But what we currently run is an event on one Sunday morning a month, when people pitch up around 10am at the church hall, where a light breakfast is available, music is playing, and Sunday papers are scattered around on small tables. There is a children's activity table for those children who want it, and most do. After a while the person who is leading will begin something like a 40-minute presentation which usually includes a mix of live music, a couple of film clips which provide the basis for a simple message using non-religious language, and activities such as quizzes. There is nothing particularly new or ground-breaking in the concept, but for us it is full of life, and I did like the comment of one person leaving a recent Soul Breakfast who said, 'I've had enough laughter today to keep me going for the week!' The laughter on that occasion, incidentally, was mostly about my anguished attempts to get the film clip to work, which resulted in people either seeing or hearing the film, but seldom the two together. I comforted myself with a comment I heard Robert Warren make once, that one of the marks of a healthy church is that it can laugh when things go wrong!

Soul Breakfast is just one of thousands of Fresh Expressions of church life that are springing up around the country, all starting from a common ambition: to create a church event where the un-churched can feel at home. When they feel at home, they will lose their normal and very understandable fears about church and be freed to be themselves, with their questions, their insights, and their wisdom. It is into this context that we can then invite the Spirit to make his presence felt, and though he is, of course, present everywhere, the dropping of defences increases the likelihood of his presence being felt. It is my experience that an increasing number of congregations are showing a willingness to break out of their set ways of doing things and to risk launching into such radically different expressions of church.

The Fresh Expressions movement is a growing force in the church, and I don't think anyone knows quite where it will lead, but my growing sense is that in 20 years' time the church into which I was ordained in 1978 will be extraordinarily different, because its life will no longer be shaped by the needs of its members but primarily by the mission context in which we live. I hear the word of the Lord originally on the lips of the exiled prophet now addressed to us in our post-Christendom exile: 'Do not remember the former things, or consider the things of old. I am about to do a new thing' (Isaiah 43:18–19a), and the key for us, as it was for Isaiah, is that searching question in verse 19, 'Do you not *perceive* it?' There is the old saying, 'There's none so blind as those that will not see', and I fear there are many in the church, as well as some fearful parts of me, that are very reluctant to open their eyes and see. But the situation is so critical that we will have to do this Isaiah work of not just seeing but really perceiving.

To grieve and to hope

I need to return to one of my mentors, Walter Brueggemann. 'Only grief permits newness,' I hear him saying over and over again, and it is a section heading in his *Hopeful Imagination*.[35] There is much to grieve, much to let go of, which is particularly hard for those of us from the long-established denominations, where our history has always been felt to be such a strength. But grieving is not about dismissing the past and certainly not about rubbishing it. In fact the past is crucially important, and the final section of Brueggemann's book is headed 'Only memory allows possibility'. In the middle of Isaiah's 'Book of Consolation' (chapters 40—55, often referred to as 'Deutero-Isaiah' or 'Second Isaiah' to indicate that it is written in exile as a sequel to the pre-exilic 'First Isaiah'), we get chapter 51, which starts off, 'Look to the rock from which you were hewn.' The prophet calls the people to look back to Abraham and Sarah, but he does so not to give them a nostalgic view of the good old days, but a resource for renewal, because right after the reference to Abraham and Sarah he writes:

For the Lord will comfort Zion;
he will comfort all her waste places,
and will make her wilderness like Eden,
her desert like the garden of the Lord;
joy and gladness will be found in her,
thanksgiving and the voice of song. (v. 3)

During times of turbulence and change, we need to look back to our stories of faith as a resource for renewal. At St Paul's I have often gone back to the beginning of this church's story, which started when the Revd James Pratt, the young curate of the neighbouring St Alkmund's Church, had the courage to start a Sunday school in the burgeoning housing development for railway workers in Chester Green, and then found funds to build a church and become its first priest till he died tragically in his early 30s. St Paul's has been built on such an inspiring vision, and we draw from that story. History can be a dynamic source of renewal. At the same time, for those who have been part of churches for more than a few years, there is grieving work to be done, particularly where significant changes have happened. As already mentioned, for those who are old enough to remember church as it once was, change can be immensely painful, and to move into a new phase of church life will demand serious grieving, a journey that some find too hard to make. Such grieving represents a proper respect for the past with a celebration of all that was good in it, although it may well involve a depth of sorrow that a phase of life that felt so good has now been and gone and can never return. But good grieving enables us to let go of our need to return, and helps us have the strength to walk into a new future.

Therapeutically, there has to be a process of stepping back to reflect on what has been, and then letting go of it, so as to be free to perceive the new. Indeed it is impossible to see a new vision if we can't free ourselves from an overriding hankering after the past. Those of us who are part of an ancient church may be very aware of our past. We walk down our churchyard paths and pass the gravestones of those who worshipped in our church and forged faith in the communities they served. We walk through our porches and often become aware that generations before us have stood where we have stood. We listen to those elderly folk who have worshipped in the church all their lives, and they remind us of those days when the Sunday school was packed and the balconies were regularly filled, crowds flocked to Evensong, and the vicar did all the work (and did it *so* well, they often remind us). And from time to time you catch a rather wistful look crossing the face of a parishioner, which says something to the effect that 'all we need is to get back to that good and glorious past', after which the eyes fall as they realise the grim reality that the vicar is progressive and is threatening another Fresh Expression...

New Zealand-born theologian, priest and anthropologist Gerald Arbuckle has written *Grieving for Change* (interestingly subtitled 'A Spirituality for Refounding Gospel Communities'), which emphasises the need to grieve properly if we are to embrace the new. Quoting the Latin poet Ovid, who wrote, 'Suppressed grief suffocates', he starts his book with a story from his childhood in the 1940s:

As a little boy of nine, I would deliver newspapers daily to subscribers in my small village in New Zealand. Each day I would meet an elderly Christian Maori Chief, who would be standing silently before a tribal meeting house faced with wooden carvings depicting his ancestors and the former greatness of his culture of pre-colonial days. He would break from his contemplation to greet me warmly but gently.

I looked forward each day to that smile and being treated as though I were an elder myself. Only later did I realise the source of his warmth and why he would stand before the carvings every day. He was grieving over the loss of the identity and sense of belonging to his people. Yet as he pondered this loss, sometimes even in tears, a new life would take hold of him. He would identify the sufferings of his people with those of Christ and believe that through the Saviour's resurrection he and his tribe would discover a new heart, a new strength. New leaders would emerge to evoke a revitalised sense of tribal self-worth through ways radically different from those of their ancestors. He did not know when this would happen. But the more he acknowledged the death of the old, the more he hoped.[36]

This Maori chief was engaging in a most therapeutic piece of theology. He was owning the grief of losing a culture that had meant so much to him and his ancestors. He took the pain of this to the cross, and not only his pain but, in a priestly way, he took the suffering of his people to the cross, for he knew that here was the place where grieving could be transformed into resurrection hope.

For those of us who are keen to move on with a fresh vision, it can feel very frustrating to give time to those who need to grieve, but all of us probably have things that we need to let go of to be truly open to a new hope. This is not just about a few traditionalists letting go of much cherished ways—modern Charismatics can find it just as difficult! Churches can be stuck in ways of worshipping that were established in the 1980s and '90s, and New Church leaders are often very aware of this. To embrace hope, there is likely to be some grieving along the way to enable us to perceive the new. Brueggemann is convinced that grieving is an essential part of discovering hope. Drawing from the words of Jeremiah, another exilic prophet, he writes:

Real hope comes not in tough-minded histrionics but precisely in, with and under grief. When there is real hope, it will not be found among his brazen colleagues, who will by then be reduced to muteness. It will be Jeremiah who is the voice of suffered hope... Eventually we realize that nobody else could hope, except for those who grieve.[37]

As I write, I realise that the matter is far from straightforward in my own soul. I may appear to be one entirely open to innovation and change, but catch me on some days, and there's nothing I want more than something nice, solid and familiar in which I can rest and feel safe. I can't deny that there is a piece of me that fully understands John Betjeman, in his *Summoned By Bells*, who finds St Ervan's partly ruined church in Cornwall, where the old Rector invites him in for a cup of tea after evensong and then upbraids him, accusing him of wanting religion to be mostly singing hymns and feeling comfortable inside—an accusation that Betjeman freely confesses to be true.[38]

In a fast-changing world, warmth and comfort have high value. Sometimes I reflect on my ancestors, those figures from the past to whom I am related, whom I have never met, yet who, through the family connection, may still have their influence in my life. I think of my grandfather's grandfather, the Revd James Mitton, who died in 1852 having been the perpetual curate of the small village of Thornthwaite in North Yorkshire for 49 years, and I think 'perpetual' is as good a word as any to describe this span of ministry. I have my days when I envy him! Life must have been extremely straightforward and simple, compared with today. I can't imagine he ever had to worry about varying his Evensongs to make the church more accessible and, for many, religion probably was about singing hymns and feeling comfortable. I have a portrait of his wife, Jane, and she clutches her Book of Common Prayer with her thin hand and peers at me over her half-moon glasses with a concerned look at my Fresh Expressions tendencies, and I catch myself feeling guilty. James and Jane were devoted to delivering a very stable ministry in a world that was changing fast, even though the culture remained solidly Christian.

They had two sons, Welbury and Joseph, who, like their father, were ordained at a young age, and it seems one of them at least was made of rather different stuff. Welbury was born on 29 November 1805 and ordained when he was 22. He became the Vicar of the new parish of St Paul's, Manningham, in Bradford and, like his father, was in for the long haul because he stayed there until he was 76. But during his time he built the church and then enlarged it twice as the congregation swelled. He also built a vicarage, a Sunday school and a school and then oversaw two church plants, St Mark's and St Luke's. Whatever spare time he had was devoted to the Church Mission Society and the British and Foreign Bible Society. This was the heyday of Victorian church life, which was utterly given to mission and expansion. His son, Henry, my great-grandfather, was ordained in 1860 and also built churches in the north-east, in Heaton and Bishop Auckland, until he broke down through overwork and stepped back from church leadership. But he was not idle, for he devoted himself to serious fund-raising and through his endeavours 45 churches and mission rooms were built.

This story, this 'looking back to the rock from which I was hewn', is, of course, very inspiring. It tells me that I am part of a church that has known periods of extraordinary vision and imagination for mission. My clerical ancestors were not exceptional: they were typical of the 19th-century church. Although it was the heyday of Christendom, nonetheless they were working in a time of colossal change, just as we are today. We may be critical of some of the ways they went about things, but we cannot doubt their courage and vision, and as such they serve to inspire us today.

James, Welbury and Henry all have their influence in my life as I am a mix of conservative and progressive, but I have no doubt that, despite my nervous interest in comfort and safety, the stronger current in my life is the one that moves towards creativity and adventure, and I carry a strong conviction that the only way the church I serve and love is likely to become thoroughly mission-shaped is now through daring exploration and risk-taking. Brueggemann, linking our current cultural situation with that of the Babylonian exiles, believes that two wonderful things happened for the people in exile: they discovered new faith, and they ventured into 'astonishing theological creativity'.[39] I always enjoy the titles of Brueggemann's books and none more so than *Deep Memory, Exuberant Hope*, for these words summarise the Isaiah 51 conviction that if we use deep memory well it can be a pathway to exuberant hope. Long before Fresh Expressions was thought of, Brueggemann was already imagining that the development of church life included a rush of creative ideas. In *Deep Memory, Exuberant Hope* he writes, 'This may be a time to replicate our exilic mothers and fathers, who believed that the way into a healed future was to let many voices and many visions play, without needing to force all into one.'[40]

I have no doubt of the truth of these words, and the sheer variety of ideas that I witness in Fresh Expressions is witness to this. It seems to me that when such new ventures don't work, it is because someone is trying to copy what they have seen in one place and replicate it in another. What is required is a much deeper listening to discern what is right for this particular situation, for this particular people, at this particular time. I am therefore expecting fast-moving and fast-changing, creative and imaginative expressions of church springing up all over the place in the coming years, each of which is designed to help the unchurched find a place of belonging where they can discover fully and wonderfully that they are beloved by God and experience the power of the Spirit bringing life to their wilderness places.

A home for all people

It is perhaps not surprising that the time when we see Jesus at his most angry is in the temple Court of the Gentiles, an episode reported in all four Gospels (see, for example, Matthew 21:12–16), which suggests it made a strong impression on the minds of the first Christians. Each evangelist tells of Jesus entering the Court of the Gentiles, a large part of the temple complex that Gentiles were permitted to use for their worship. It was a specially designated place, therefore, for those who were not fully 'in', yet who were to be made welcome. What outraged Jesus was that the commercial side of the temple's affairs had filled this space, so that there was little room left for Gentiles who wished to worship. The whole religious paraphernalia had effectively pushed the 'outsiders' well outside. In Matthew's Gospel, after his angry outburst, with tables and chairs scattered all over the place and worried money-changers feeling in the dust for their coins and keeping well out of the way of this wild rabbi, the blind and the lame shuffle their way to Jesus, filling the sacred space he has created, and in the midst of broken table legs, scattered coins and pigeon feathers he stretches out his hand and heals them. Moreover, as a background chorus to the whole thing, a load of children appear from nowhere singing their Hosannas at the tops of their voices. It is a scene that would reduce the most hard-hearted to tears. Well, almost all the most hard-hearted, because sure enough there were some stone-hearted chief priests and teachers of the law who quickly came on the scene with their complaints.

Is it too much to relate this to modern church life? The parallels are obvious: we create our 'temples' to be places that are well suited to our kind of worship and our kind of people. We can claim that we are welcoming, but when it comes down to it, we are reluctant to change our ways to accommodate others. We know, perhaps only too well, that if we become too accommodating it will only attract those who are likely to be emotionally, if not literally, lame and blind, and we just haven't the resources to cope, and we imagine they would be a very disturbing presence. Besides, we might think, we have to give so much of our energy and space nowadays to fund-raising, just to keep the church going and the building in good shape. We don't really have time for real outsiders. As regards children, we would, of course, love to have more of them in church, but really they are so badly behaved nowadays and some of them, well, their language is quite inappropriate for a Sunday morning...

It is worth pausing, on a Sunday morning or whenever it is you have your main act of worship, and imagining Jesus coming into your building. Then imagine you take the risk of going up close to him and, looking as hard as you dare, try to see the expression on his face. The chances are that most of us will be taken aback, because Jesus had such a compassionate, generous, overwhelming love for outsiders that if we are not making space for them we will see deep sorrow in his face and a questioning as to why we have not been more welcoming. After that famous cleansing incident in the temple, it is clear that for a few blessed moments, before the chief priests and doctors of the law returned things to 'normal', Jesus made the temple home for the dispossessed and ostracised, so it was no wonder that beggars were healed and children sang out.

Another key story for me in relation to all of this is that of Pentecost. I really can't imagine what it was like for those first disciples after Jesus ascended into heaven. He had been coming and going in what must have been a most disturbing way for six weeks, and then he made a final departure from the Mount of Olives, basically leaving them to it, but promising them the Holy Spirit. Even the most theologically astute of them might have struggled to know quite what this meant, but they did the only sensible thing when faced with a puzzling situation: they stayed together and they prayed (Acts 1:13–14). A sense of community was surely growing among them in those days and we are told that there were about 120 of them (v. 15) who were doing what Jesus had told them, which was to wait, while Jerusalem started to fill up with foreigners from all over the known world. On the great festival day of Pentecost, while Jerusalem was seething, that which Jesus said would happen did happen—the Holy Spirit arrived and all that the disciples experienced when Jesus was physically with them was now back again, but more so. The coming of the Spirit was marked by billowing wind and fire from heaven, and as if that wasn't peculiar enough, the disciples found they started to speak words that were quite unfamiliar to them. A hundred and twenty once-normal people, now in a blazing, billowing upper room, speaking words that meant precious little to them! The full significance of this experience emerges in the next part of the story.

The streets outside this house were a frenzy of activity as visitors had come from all over the world for the festival. There were Parthians, Medians and Elamites and goodness knows who else from all kinds of places far away speaking languages that were not remotely like the disciples' mother tongue. They were all there, bustling their way to the temple, until they passed near that house, from which they heard something they never imagined they would hear: they heard their own languages. You can imagine the scene: a Median woman is stopped in her tracks as she hears her language spoken perfectly; a blind child from Mesopotamia, clinging to his mother's hand, hears someone speaking his language perfectly and beautifully; the rugged Cretan, swaying a little after too much wine, steadies himself by a stone wall and hears a woman's voice speaking his language. And as they all listen, they hear about 'God's deeds of power' (Acts 2:11), and we can only speculate about which particular deeds they were proclaiming. Those first hearers would have made enquiries and discovered this was not an all-nations meeting with reps from every country but actually a bunch of fairly uneducated people from Galilee. Human nature being what it is, it is not surprising that some imagined the best and some the worst

(vv. 12–13). Those who imagined the best heard the good news and we are told that about 3000 people were baptised (v. 41).

The key part of this story, which is often considered to mark the birth of the church, is the fact that one of the first consequences of the Holy Spirit visiting this group of 120 young Christians was that they took to speaking other people's languages. However you understand this event, the fact is that unsuspecting Parthians, Egyptians and the rest of them heard the great deeds of God *in their own languages*. If we regard this story as the birth of the church, then we must expect church to be a community of Spirit-filled people who are given an instinct to understand other languages (if not literally, then metaphorically) and make the mighty deeds of God known in that language. It is a story that is full of significance for us today, as we find ourselves in small communities in the midst of a very busy world full of a multitude of different cultures. We carry the good news of the love of God, and we are offered by God the gift of the Holy Spirit. As we pray and worship together, we should expect that one way or another we instinctively find ourselves drawn to cultures that are not our own and find ways of proclaiming the good news, not in our language but in theirs.

Although we have a long way to go, I like to think that our local Soul Breakfast service at St Paul's is an attempt to share the things of God in the language of the young families living locally. I believe the Holy Spirit has helped us in trying to understand and speak this language. Some may worry that in doing this we are no longer true to who we really are, but the Holy Spirit is the one who leads us into all truth (John 16:13). The Holy Spirit leads us also into authenticity, which means being truly ourselves.

The search for authenticity

Speaking with those who are planting churches for young adult groups, I am told that when young adults do make their way to a church the key quality they are looking for is authenticity. The church makes extremely bold claims of faith and holds to such ideals as loving our enemies, and doing good to those that hate us, and loving God with all our hearts, and caring for the poor, and siding with those treated unjustly. People want to see evidence that we practise what we preach, and so they should. If we say one thing and live another, we have little authority, let alone authenticity.

I suspect another reason for the desire to find authenticity in the life of the church is something to do with integrating what some may term the 'sacred' and the 'secular'. In other words, many people are anxious about the Christian faith because their experience of Christians has led them to assume that the more Christian you are, the more holy you are, and the more holy you are, the more removed you are from this world. But people who live in this world, by and large, don't want to be removed from it. They want to know how to live an authentic and full life *in* it while they are here. They respond more eagerly to those who show every sign of living *in* this world and being connected with it, yet have a quality of life that makes them different. Early on in my Christian experience, I was taught a song which encouraged us to turn our eyes upon Jesus, and in so doing the things of the world would grow 'strangely dim'. Though it was a much-loved song at the time, it implied that to look at Jesus takes us more and more away from a murky and difficult world that causes us to sin so much. A rather different spirituality is now emerging which is altogether more integrated and indeed incarnational, and it is about engaging fully in this world, yet at the same time experiencing the glory and grace of Jesus.

Another measure of authenticity is the ability to accept people and situations when things go wrong. Home is a safe place if we feel we still belong in it even when we have made mistakes. Once, when I was about eight years old, I found a fire extinguisher in the cupboard under the stairs. I was fascinated by this red cylinder: what would happen if I pulled the trigger? What kind of stuff could possibly come out of it that had the amazing ability to put out a fire? There was only one way to find out—if I could just press the trigger very, very quickly, I would see a little of this miraculous substance. I squeezed and squeezed until finally there was a click and out shot a strong-smelling fine white powder. But then I made the dreadful discovery: once you pressed the trigger, there was no way to stop the outpouring of this pungent, sticky powder. Out it came, on and on, filling the hall, the landing, the rooms with their welcoming open doors, adhering to furniture, carpets, lampshades and curtains. And then, through the white mist, like a rising sun on a foggy day, appeared the red face of my mother! For those moments as I ran in terror to the garden shed, home did not feel like home. And yet, by night-time as I settled into my bed, with the mops drying in the kitchen and my mother finally relaxing in front of the telly, I rested deeply. I knew everything was all right, because, despite my faults, my home could still hold me. I was indeed fortunate to be in a home that made space for my failings.

If church is to be a true home, it has to provide a sense of sanctuary for all of us even when we have failed in one way or another. I sense a new longing for authenticity not just in the expectations of the unchurched but among church members themselves. It is just too exhausting trying to pretend to be very holy and constantly overflowing with confident and radiant faith. If church is to be home in the sense of being a place where I know I am beloved for who I am, a place where I can be free of fear and shame, where I will always belong, then I have to be able to have my bad days, share my struggles of faith and my battles with my shortcomings. It is not that church is where everyone turns a blind eye to shortcomings and unsociable behaviour. I know I need direction, challenge and discipline, just as much as I need a place of safety. Without those I am less likely to grow, and a home is a place for growing. I grew up in my childhood home, and the home of church is the place where I continue to grow up to become all that I am meant to be in this world.

To build a community that provides the environment for this kind of growing up demands a great deal from the leaders of that community, for they more than anyone will have to model authenticity. If we as leaders are not modelling being fully ourselves as we lead our churches, what hope is there for the church members? But if we can take risks and lead as who we really are rather than what we think we should be, or what people need us to be, we give permission for others to follow on the same journey. When a church community commits to a way of authenticity, visitors to the church will sense this, and some inner longing will stir in them, that homing instinct which makes them wonder whether here, at last, is a place on earth where they can be themselves.

The acid test in all of this comes when being myself happens to involve an issue that someone else finds offensive or challenging. An example of this is the currently intensely discussed and hotly debated issue of homosexuality. What if someone who is homosexual seeks to join a church that is exclusively or predominantly heterosexual? The homosexual unchurched person may arrive and for a time keep their orientation secret for fear of rejection. What happens when that person finally plucks up the courage to let it be known that they are different and, in some churches, not only different but 'wrong' in the minds of some members? Suddenly something that was only 'an issue' becomes personal for the church. The commitment to authenticity and the freedom to be ourselves is challenged. Anxiety grows and people may start talking of 'policies' as a convenient way of sorting a delicate problem. What has to grow, of course, is relationship. The only way forward is for us to really listen to one another, and listening to someone who is different from us and who holds very different views from ours is one of the hardest listening tasks, for it carries the very real risk that somewhere down the line, values that lie deep in me and my community will be challenged. Homes can break up because of this: a son or daughter grows in their conviction about a particular issue, and the family party line is contested, people feel betrayed or misunderstood and tempers rise, and no one listens because they are too busy shouting their own views. There are times when it is far from comfortable in a home, but a good home is a place of belonging that has become so strong that even the most contentious subjects can be discussed with safety, and all members are willing to journey beyond their assumptions.

It is becoming clear, then, that if churches are to be places of belonging, true homes where all can come to find out that they are beloved on the earth, this will not guarantee a tranquil, settled existence. Far from it! It is much more likely that home in this regard will be the place that provides safety not for settling but for exploration and fresh encounter. A good home is a starting point, a base camp, from which real adventuring can take place, and a safe place of belonging that is always there for us to return to.

Every now and again something happens that enables me to see what it is like when church is truly a home. It may be in the church where I worship or in one I am visiting or have heard about. As I come to the end of this chapter, I find myself thinking about a man called Frank who was an elderly member of St Paul's when I first arrived. Frank was one of those people who always evoked a definite response from people. In short, they either loved or hated him! 'Hating', in all honesty, is far too strong a word, but his partiality for the bottle, his outspoken forthright views and his tendency to swear fairly freely and loudly did not endear him to the local community. In truth, Frank was, like any of us, a mix of good and bad, but for me the good was by far the greater part of him, and the bad was to some degree understandable because grief had got the better of him and he had never really recovered from the loss of both his first and second wives through untimely death. When I got to know Frank he was not in the best of health, but his resolute spirit and twinkling humour were immediately endearing. He was fearless as far as I could see, which meant he had little care for what people thought of him, and scant regard for his own or others' safety as he rode his mobility scooter erratically and at some speed around the streets of Derby. His great love was singing, and though his ageing voice was somewhat croaky, he would sometimes catch us at the back of church and sing us a few lines of a Frank Sinatra song, and in those moments we got a glimpse of his talent that at one time in his life would have been truly impressive. To my great admiration, the folks at St Paul's loved Frank and took him to their hearts.

Towards the end of his life he was quite frail and I particularly remember one Christmas morning when he arrived and, after parking his scooter, awkwardly shifted himself into his normal pew at the back of church. In the service I spoke about Christmas gifts and about the gifts and talents God has given us, which are for us to share. I had also mentioned this the previous week and invited people to bring poetry, songs, handiwork, paintings and so on to church to show us, which many did. Frank knew his gift was singing, and he asked to sing us a Christmas carol. We decided that after Communion would be the best time. With some difficulty he came up the aisle to the altar to take his Communion, and having received the gifts of bread and wine, he made his way back to share his gift with us. He decided to stop by my seat, the vicar's stall at the front of church, and planted himself firmly in it. After all had received Communion, I said slightly anxiously, 'Frank will now share with us a gift of a Christmas carol.' He immediately pulled his tired body up in the priest's stall and the sound of the creaking of the ancient wood gave way to his shaky voice as he started singing the first verse of 'Away in a Manger'. By the second verse he had found his old form, and people were spellbound. The organist found the key he was singing in and accompanied him. Beginning the last verse, he looked up to the vaulted ceiling of the chancel as he sang to his God 'to fit him for heaven to live with him there'. He then slumped noisily back into the stall, and with the sweat shining on his forehead and his hands twitching from the exertion of holding himself up, he looked at me and with his loud voice asked, 'Was I good?' I turned to the congregation and asked, 'Was Frank good?' to which the spontaneous response was loud cheering and clapping. 'I can do Frank Sinatra, too!' cried Frank, now elated, but we agreed that that was best left for another day. As I watched Frank precariously meander down the church to his mobility scooter, with people patting him on the back, I was in no doubt that in those moments he was living in his homeland and, in so doing, welcomed us all in. Church was for him a safe place and, despite his many faults, it was where he could sing his song.

It wasn't very long after that December day that I was leading Frank's funeral service at the local crematorium, and as the curtain closed around the coffin and the small scattered congregation listened to Frank Sinatra's 'My Way' belting out over the chapel sound system, I thought of our Frank finally and fully healed in a homeland where he could sing forever to his heart's content, and the tears of grief were being wiped from his eyes and death was no more. God had fitted him for the heaven that was now his home. It is to this homeland that we now turn our thoughts.

For reflection

If you are a churchgoer, to what extent is church truly home for you? How much does it manage to be home for visitors? What needs to happen to make it more like home? And if you are not a churchgoer, what would you look for in a church to make it feel home for you?

Reuben's story (6)

What most of us disliked about this Rabbi was the fact that he had precious little regard for the things that give us a proper sense of order. We don't make these laws up just to make life harder for people. If you want a secure society, people need to know where they stand. They need to know what is right and what is wrong, but there seemed to be a lot of grey areas in the teaching of this Rabbi. What we found the people really needed was black and white, not murky grey. It was his love for the sinners that really made us angry. To be so accepting of them was quite intolerable. Take that woman the other day, for example. Poor old Mattathias—his wife was actually found in the bed of another man. Well, we were all fairly sure that was the case, anyway. There was more or less enough evidence, and the way she tried to protest her innocence was surely proof of her guilt. She was that kind of woman. The men who found her decided to take her to this Rabbi just to see what he would say.

By our law the woman should have been stoned to death— no question. Would this Rabbi uphold the law like any decent rabbi would? Imagine our horror when he let her off—not even a pebble was thrown at her! Most of the people went away murmuring that he clearly had no morals at all. But one of my friends there, a really good Pharisee called Elkiah, told me how he did the strangest thing. He wrote something in the dust, and when Elkiah went to read it, he said it made his blood turn cold.

He said he could never tell me what that writing said, but the Rabbi might as well have written in that dust the whole story of his life.

I was feeling a bit like that now. This annoying Rabbi seemed to have an unnerving way of seeing right into you, and that was the problem with the stories he told. If you weren't very careful they would catch you out, which is why we all had to be on our guard. He was poisoning the minds of the people. Well, at least, that was the official line. I was thinking about this 'official line' as he drew to the end of the story of the wayward son. I struggled with the thought of all that celebration for the wicked boy returning home. I have to admit, though, that while I officially disapproved of that, something inside me also wanted to dance and sing and join the party. I felt split in two, between the well-behaved, disapproving bit and a much freer bit that was rejoicing and wanted to run off to Crete for an adventure. It was as if there was a wrestling match going on inside me. Who was going to win?

Then he took us all by surprise. We thought he had finished the story and people started to get ready to go, when he told us about the older brother. I must admit I had hardly noticed this character when he had been mentioned at the start of the story. The Rabbi told us that while the party was going on, the older brother had been working in the field, and when he heard all the commotion and celebration, he asked what was happening. Well, this was one bit of the story that did not surprise me at all. Quite understandably this older brother, who had been the model son his entire life, was very upset when he saw his wayward brother being doted on, while all *his* good works seemed to have been completely ignored. This Galilean Rabbi was actually implying that the older brother should join the party, because he ought to be delighted that his wrong-doing good-for-nothing brother had come home!

And that was the end of the story. The last words, spoken by the father to the older son, were 'He was lost and is found', and those words would not leave my mind. People began to move away while a small group gathered around the Rabbi, as the sun dazzled us through the lower branches of the fig tree on its slow descent toward the distant hills. Shemaiah sighed. I knew he wanted to talk with me, but I just wanted to be quiet and collect my thoughts. Wherever this Rabbi went, there seemed to be parties. People like those prostitutes in the front row, or that woman caught in adultery, or that tax collector who was apparently one of his disciples now: they seemed to be living in a celebration that I could never be part of. Or could I? Something in me recoiled at the thought of being that older brother standing on the edge with his rules and regulations— but, of course, that is who I was. And yet, this story had shown me that I was not just the older brother but the younger brother as well. As the Rabbi told the story, I was away to my far-off land, I came to myself, and I allowed myself to believe that the Almighty could forgive me even that dreadful thing I once did. According to this story, he was a very different father from my own. He was one who was more interested in welcoming his children home than in sending them into exile. Would I join the party or would I stay outside? I could hear my father; I recalled the harsh words he had said about this Rabbi from Nazareth. I swear he would have been more than happy to stone him to death if he could or put him on one of those terrible crosses the Romans use. And my good friend Shemaiah—he did not care much for him. But there was that look in that Galilean's eyes, wasn't there? How was I going to choose?

I was standing very still, with others moving around me, and I became aware of someone putting a hand on my shoulder and a woman's voice said, 'Reuben?' I turned round, but the setting sun was blazing behind this figure so I could not see her face. I frowned in the bright light and shielded my eyes with my hand. I recognised the voice as she said again, 'Reuben?' and then I knew without any doubt who it was. It was my sister Judith and she was standing right in front of me, and she was using my name.

Chapter 6

Longing for home

Browsing through a Christian magazine a little while ago, I chanced upon an article that referred to a man called John who, we were told, had 'been called home in 1997'. It's a phrase I'd seen dozens of times, and I knew full well it was a Christian euphemism to indicate that this person was dead. It somehow feels altogether kinder and less sharp to say that he had gone home than to use the cold and stark word 'died'. But on this occasion, as I read the article and knew the man who had been 'called home', I appreciated the fact that the writer wasn't using the phrase as a euphemism but was actually pointing to a theological, and to some extent emotional, reality. John was now 'home' in a way that he wasn't while he was alive. The word 'home' used in this way means a place you never finally reach during your lifetime. You get to it only through the gateway of death.

What does it really mean, though? If an angel turned up in my study this afternoon and, after reassuring me and giving me whatever angels use as smelling salts to revive me, said, 'Michael, I'm pleased to tell you that the Lord is calling you *home*,' I'd have a mixture of feelings. Instinctively I'd want to pack a case of special belongings, photos of my family, letters from my wife and children, Mark Knopfler's *Sailing to Philadelphia* album, my journals, one of Buechner's books, and the Wisden *Cricketers' Almanack* detailing the famous Ashes victory of 2005. In fact, given time, the case could get quite full. But the look on the angel's face would soon tell me that none of this was allowed. I just had to come as I was, because the home I was heading for wouldn't involve any of that stuff. And there lies a bit of a problem. For, as wonderful as the promise of the new home might be, I can't help feeling that uppermost in my mind at that moment would be a feeling not of delight at being called home, but rather regret at being called away from everything I have come to see as marking out what I know as home.

Ask me for a gut response about what home means for me, and I'll tell you that it is to do with being close to my wife, my children, my grandchildren, my wider family, my friends, the house where I live, my town and this beautiful blue, green, brown and white spinning globe that is the home for all of us in the days of life allotted to us. How could somewhere that doesn't include at least a few of these possibly be called my 'home'? Maybe if I were, say, 98 and most of those to whom I have been close in this life had been 'called home', the news from that angel would indeed sound like a journey to a destination that really would feel like home. But at the moment, even though some very dear friends and family have gone on ahead of me, there are still too many of them here to make anywhere else sound much like home.

And what if I were a child who, as was the case with my Uncle Horace, did not live to see his second birthday, being taken from his devoted mother's arms to be met by unknown ancestors in the celestial home? Or if I were a 19-year-old soldier with all my adult life ahead of me, and an enemy bullet sent me 'home'? How do I feel about that idea? So long as this eternal home is presented as something quite unrelated to the home I inhabit now, there will always be a sense within me that it couldn't possibly be the place of true belonging that I want it to be.

When my friend Phil Baggaley wrote his wonderful musical *City of Gold*, based to some extent on Bunyan's *Pilgrim's Progress*, bringing together songs, poems and readings about heaven, he included a poem by Adrian Plass simply called 'Heaven'. The poem starts 'When I'm in heaven, tell me there'll be kites to fly', and it goes on to express a hope that heaven will include bits of this world and this life that have felt like heaven to us in our days here on earth. It finishes with the lines:

And if there is some harm in laying earthly hope at heaven's door
Or in this saying so,
Have mercy on my foolishness, dear Lord,
I love this world you made—it's all I know. [41]

And yet, for all our love of this world we know, instinctively we also know that it is not the whole story. We love our homes, our families, our planet, and yet we know that even the most secure homes are always under threat: circumstances may mean we lose houses that have become home for us; breakdowns in relationships mean we lose closeness with friends and families; planners and builders can make our towns less like home; pollution and war threaten the security of our planet; worst of all, death steals from us those whose presence made us feel at home. Because all the homes of this world are vulnerable, there is another homing instinct that makes us long for a home that will not be shaken and a place of utter security that none can disturb.

The apostle Paul, in his correspondence with the Christians in Corinth, writes with feeling about his longing for home. He refers to this in 2 Corinthians 5:1–10, and I like Eugene Petersen's paraphrase of some of these verses in THE MESSAGE:

Compared to what's coming, living conditions around here seem like a stopover in an unfurnished shack, and we're tired of it! We've been given a glimpse of the real thing, our true home, our resurrection bodies! The Spirit of God whets our appetite by giving us a taste of what's ahead. He puts a little of heaven in our hearts so that we'll never settle for less.

That's why we live with such good cheer. You won't see us drooping our heads or dragging our feet! Cramped conditions here don't get us down. They only remind us of the spacious living conditions ahead. It's what we trust in but don't yet see that keeps us going. Do you suppose a few ruts in

*the road or rocks in the path are going to stop us? When the time comes,
we'll be plenty ready to exchange exile for homecoming.*

Paul is not the only New Testament writer to see heaven as our true
home, with our life here on earth as an exile by comparison. The
writer to the Hebrews also uses this theme in the chapter about
the heroes of faith. Hebrews 11 begins with the well-known words,
'Now faith is the assurance of things hoped for, the conviction of
things not seen.' The writer then runs through a list of faith-filled
people starting with Abel. In the midst of this list, we have:

*All of these died in faith without having received the promises, but from
a distance they saw and greeted them. They confessed that they were
strangers and foreigners on the earth, for people who speak in this way
make it clear that they are seeking a homeland. If they had been thinking
of the land that they had left behind, they would have had opportunity
to return. But as it is, they desire a better country, that is, a heavenly
one. Therefore God is not ashamed to be called their God; indeed, he has
prepared a city for them.* (vv. 13–16)

In his book *The Longing for Home*, Frederick Buechner uses the
phrase 'homesickness of the spirit' to describe that emotion deep
inside us that hankers after something that we can't quite put our
finger on, something we can't define with any clarity, because
it is beyond our imaginings yet by no means separate from our
imaginings. He picks up the themes in Hebrews 11 and, noting the
list of faith heroes, he writes:

*How do you deal with that homesickness of the spirit… that longing for
whatever the missing thing is that keeps even the home of the present from
being the true home? I only wish I knew. All I know is that… I also sense
that something of great importance is missing which I cannot easily name
and which perhaps can never be named by any us until we find it if indeed*

it is ever to be found. In the meanwhile, like Gideon and Barak and the others, I also know the sense of sadness and lostness that comes with feeling that you are a stranger and exile on the earth and that you would travel to the ends of that earth and beyond if you thought you could ever find the homeland that up till now you have only glimpsed from afar.[42]

Exploring the subject he decides that this longing for home is a very powerful human drive that leads us into our deepest relationships of love, but even beyond that 'there lies a longing, closer to the heart of the matter still, which is the longing to be at long last where you fully belong.'[43] The homing instinct that I described at the beginning of this book therefore has another dimension. We search in this world for a place where we can be beloved on the earth, a place of belonging where we can be ourselves without fear or shame. Like the prodigal son, we have our moments of coming to our senses, making significant discoveries about ourselves and our God that lead us into the warm embrace of the welcoming Father. This is the route that leads to experiences of home in this world. But all the time we know that this life and this world will inevitably come to an end one day. Our longing therefore makes us cry out, 'There must be somewhere beyond all of this where I can be finally and for ever myself and be at home', and the focus of that hope has to be the paradise that the scriptures give us glimpses of, that our instincts suspect is somewhere, and that Barak and Gideon and the others grasped by faith, which gave them a clear conviction that such a home was not wishful thinking but actual fact.

There is a series of poems written by Stewart Henderson called 'Giant' which appears in one of his early anthologies, *A Giant's Scrapbook*.[44] In ten short poems we are introduced to this character who simply feels that there is nowhere in this world where he really fits. Everywhere he goes he is the wrong size. In the first poem, 'Giant's Morning Story', he bemoans the problems his size brings him, but then he pauses:

'Perhaps there is a city where everything works,'
sighs Giant, expectant of a usual morning being pointed at,
'a city where I am the right height.'

It is his heart's desire, his longing for home. In the poem 'Correspondence' he comes across a note that says, 'I've known you since the beginning', and when he reads this 'it makes him feel almost content'. The final poem, 'First Steps', describes how Giant finds a castle that is much larger than he is, and he instinctively feels drawn to it. He hears beautiful singing as the drawbridge lowers and invitingly lands at his feet. The poem ends with the lines:

Giant heard a voice.
It said: 'You can now enter.
This is where you will finally be the right size.'
And so Giant went into the castle.
He did not diminish,
and as he walked past pillars of flaming glass
a lover's voice spoke his name
and the singing began again.

Raymond Carver's longing was to be beloved *on the earth*, and the homing instinct is to do with this longing. But the instinct is more than the longing to be beloved on the earth, vital and important though that is. The earth is full of pointers to another world, another home, where the Lover's voice speaks our name and where we finally feel we fit in, and where nothing can spoil or destroy. There is therefore an instinct to be beloved not just on the earth but also *in heaven*.

There's a beautiful old hymn by the 19th-century American hymn writer Sanford Bennett. His violinist friend Joseph Webster was apparently a very nervous and sensitive man and prone to periods of depression. While he was in one of these dark moods

Bennett tried to cheer him up, and he replied, 'It will be all right by and by.' Though his words carried only a faint glimmer of faith and hope, it was enough for Sanford Bennett, who, without delay, put pen to paper and wrote:

There's a land that is fairer than day,
And by faith we can see it afar;
For the Father waits over the way
To prepare us a dwelling place there.

In the sweet by and by,
We shall meet on that beautiful shore;
In the sweet by and by,
We shall meet on that beautiful shore.

Webster immediately took hold of his violin and in a short time drafted a melody to match the words. It is a hymn that I have not often sung but one that I have heard in recordings, and there is something about the words and melody that awakens my instinct for a heavenly home. We perhaps all know hymns, songs or poems that move us in such a way that we are alerted to this longing for a home beyond the homes of this world. The word in Sandford Bennett's lyric that catches my eye is 'faith', for what becomes clear in all of this is the Hebrews 11 quality of faith that provides a peculiar and wonderful kind of vision that can perceive what we can only hope for at the moment. Faith is the assurance of things hoped for, a kind of inner sense that things unseen do exist. 'Faith,' says Christopher Bryant in his book *The River Within*, 'has been called a kind of intuitive knowledge, an intuitive awareness of the unseen. Intuition has been described as perception by way of the unconscious.'[45] I have always found this a helpful way of understanding faith, as I like to think of it as being located in that instinctive, intuitive part of ourselves, and this is one very good reason to take care of it.

The homing instinct makes us long for a place of belonging where we are free to be ourselves without fear or shame. It is the sense of being beloved that shifts the awful burden of shame, and it is faith that counters our tendency to fear. When I started writing this book I was caught in a very literal story to do with home. Having taken the decision to move into a freelance way of life, my wife and I had to vacate the vicarage in which we were living. We owned a small house and we came to the decision that the best plan was to sell it and buy somewhere a little bigger to provide an office for my new work. And so, in the midst of the credit crunch crisis and gloomy prognostications about the housing market, we put our little house on the market and set about searching for a new home. We were told that moving house is one of the most stressful of human activities, and why not? We are talking about our home, which is so fundamental to our sense of well-being and security. The days went past and it was proving hard to sell our house. We had seen the house we wanted to buy and loved it and longed for it. The vicarage in which we were living was needed by the diocese for another occupant, and the autumn days went by and the deadline by which we had to vacate approached. The experience evoked all kinds of fears in me and when my fears dominated, my faith shrivelled. In my 'fear world', the housing market, the economic climate and the mood of purchasers and vendors all became great powers determining my fate. Then I would reach out to that part of me that is capable of faith, and I would go into Isaiah 40 and preach to my doubting soul, 'The nations are but a drop in the bucket—the nations, the housing market, the solicitors and estate agents, the whole jolly lot of them are tiny compared with the hollow of the hand that holds the waters of earth' (see vv. 12–15).

I alternated restlessly and wearingly between faith and fear, and I discovered that when I was deep in my fears, the world defined by those fears was a tiny place, surrounded by a boundary fence with 'danger' on it. My fears made me doubt God's protection, his love and his competency at house transactions and they warned me to retreat to safety. But when I chose faith, I felt as if the world grew astonishingly: I could push beyond the sense of threat, the insinuating fears and the downright untruths, and on I would go into a place of trust in God, who is the God of the impossible, and I felt power entering my faint heart. One day, when I was out for a walk and saw two paragliders circling overhead, I remembered with much feeling the words of that prophet among the fearing exiles, 'but those who wait for the Lord shall renew their strength; they shall rise up with wings like eagles' (Isaiah 40:31), and for a few moments I was there, circling the skies above the cold earth of my fears, carried by the warm currents of faith.

I had imagined that such faith would produce the goods: that houses would be sold and bought at just the right time, and we would settle in our promised land. But no; there was a more mysterious path for us to tread. On the day that we expected to exchange contracts, the vendor pulled out and the sale fell through. The next days were spent dispensing with furniture that would not fit in the smaller house, and desperately adjusting plans. My deepest fears had come true: we were not entering the house of my dreams, but the house of my fears. For a time I felt as if my 'faith' world was nothing but wishful thinking.

That winter we transformed our house, and in the process it became a haven for us. My valley of weeping, of Baca, was becoming a place of springs (Psalm 84:6). Eventually we moved again and I write today in a home that feels wonderfully and fully home, not least because it has been a journey of faith to get here.

Faith is the quality that enables us to catch a tantalising glimpse of our eternal home. Yes, it is still true that if that angel turned up today and announced, 'You are coming home', I'd still feel a sorrow at leaving all that has become home for me in this world. But faith is that part of me that instinctively knows that the ultimate home is the place where, to use Giant's language, I will be the 'right size'. Faith gives me the intuitive awareness that, though I may be passing through a dark night of the soul in this world, there is a land that is 'fairer than day' that awaits me in the next. Faith also helps me, in the bright daytimes of this world, to know that the home to come is not about having to let go of all that is home now, but is, curiously and mysteriously, simply an extension of it. There is no weeping, no crying, no death (Revelation 21:4), so I need not imagine that my arrival in heaven will involve wistful glances back to this world. The two worlds will be caught up together in ways that are well beyond my mortal mind to imagine. But the homing instinct helps me to have the faith to believe it.

In C.S. Lewis' *The Last Battle*, the final book in the Narnia series, he explores this theme of heaven and he also uses this notion of home:

It was the Unicorn who summed up what everyone was feeling. He stamped his right fore-hoof on the ground and neighed and cried:

'I have come home at last! This is my real country! I belong here. This is the land I have been looking for all my life, though I never knew it till now. The reason why we loved the old Narnia is that it sometimes looked a little like this. Bree-hee-hee! Come farther up, come farther in!'[46]

The new Narnia is connected to the old Narnia. It is this connectedness of heaven and earth that I find so encouraging. I have been created to live fully in this world while at the same time my heart is set on another one, my 'real country'. It sounds paradoxical but it somehow works. The more faith helps sharpen my vision to see my eternal homeland, the more I long to see the qualities of home established in this world. In my experience, every glimpse of paradise is not about escaping this world but about wanting to make even more of it.

Homemakers in this world

This vision of the paradise home has indeed inspired many people to be homemakers in this world. Martin Luther King Jr, that man whose dream changed a nation if not a world, loved one hymn more than any other—'Precious Lord', which ends with the line, 'Take my hand, precious Lord, lead me home.'

He often invited the gospel singer Mahalia Jackson to sing it at his rallies, and at his request she sang it at his funeral in April 1968. According to Jesse Jackson, as King stood on the balcony at the Lorraine Motel in Memphis, Tennessee, he said to his musician Ben Branch, 'Ben, make sure you play "Take my hand, precious Lord" in the meeting tonight. Play it real pretty.' Those were apparently his last words before the assassin's bullet tore into his body.[47]

At first glance this favourite hymn appears a little escapist, especially when you get to the last verse, which is clearly about the ending of the day of this life and the approaching darkness of death. Yet Martin Luther King found this hymn stirred him to radical actions for justice and freedom for his people. He would have known that it had been written by Thomas Dorsey in 1932. Dorsey was a black man living in Chicago and he knew his fair share of suffering due to racial discrimination. But it was a more personal tragedy that precipitated the writing of the hymn: his beloved wife Nettie died while giving birth to a child, and the child too died shortly afterwards. In his shock and grief, Dorsey wrote this wonderfully crafted hymn of faith. He shared it with his friend, gospel singer Theodore Frye; Frye's choir sang it the next Sunday at the Ebenezer Baptist Church in Chicago, and it has been sung by choirs ever since. The vision of home expressed in this simple hymn inspired not only Martin Luther King but also countless others to bring to birth the qualities of that future home in this world, such that those who found themselves exiles in this life because of human injustice and personal tragedy would discover homelands, places of safety and belonging.

My wife and I visited Chicago during my sabbatical and, as it turned out, we were there three weeks before the American elections of 2008. The city was in a fever of excitement as their boy, Barack Obama, was in a neck-and-neck race with John McCain for the presidency. We took a sunlit bus tour around the city and our driver was a black woman who gave us a running commentary as she drove us down the wide streets beneath the vast and beautiful skyscrapers. At one point she took us past Grant Park and told us that she had recently had the privilege of singing in the Park and that she would like to sing to us now. She started singing Thomas Dorsey's hymn, and as she did so she swayed with emotion in her driving seat and I thought of Martin Luther King holding on to the song in his great, unswaying heart. As we got off the bus I saw the driver smiling but also wiping tears from her eyes, for the song was at work in her heart and not merely on her lips. Three weeks after that day we were back in the UK watching on TV the scenes from Grant Park, as Barack Obama and his family walked on to the stage to the cheers of the delighted voters, and I thought to myself that it was very likely that somewhere in that crowd there was a bus driver. I imagined her singing again that song, and I imagined she felt that her nation was now for her much more a homeland, a place of belonging. Something of the quality of the eternal home had broken through. Something of Martin Luther King's dream had come to pass.

That experience reminded me that, no matter how much I might draw closer to my own homeland in this world, there will always be those far from home, like the hurting and grieving Thomas Dorsey and the oppressed people for whom Martin Luther King gave his life. Though progress has been made, there are still far too many who live as exiles and refugees in this world and for whom there is no safe home to which they can return. There are also those who have not yet made their 'prodigal' way to that place of knowing that they are the beloved on the earth and still wander far and wide in search of belonging. I have to go back one final time to the words of Frederick Buechner, who puts it so well:

To be homeless the way people like you and me are apt to be homeless is to have homes all over the place but not to be really at home in any of

*them. To be really at home is to be really at peace, and our lives are so
intricately interwoven that there can be no real peace for any of us until
there is peace for all of us.* [48]

I know I am on my way home; I dare to believe that the Father is
as welcoming to me as the father was to that wayward son in Jesus'
parable. But every time I give thanks for my home, I am aware that
there are those who are homeless in so many different ways and,
following on from Buechner's words, so long as there is one who
is homeless in this world, a part of me is restless and not at home.
It is this, more than anything, that causes me to yearn for that day
when the welcoming Father will wipe every tear from every eye.
Again and again I need to read the verse, 'Death will be no more;
mourning and crying and pain will be no more, for the first things
have passed away' (Revelation 21:4).

The article I referred to at the beginning of this chapter said that
John was now at 'home with the Lord', a phrase used by Paul in his
correspondence with the Corinthian Christians (see 2 Corinthians
5:1–10) in the context of a discussion about this earthly body (a
'tent') and the body we will have in heaven (a 'heavenly dwelling').
As far as I can understand it, Paul here is sharing his conviction that
heaven is the place where we are 'at home with the Lord', which
implies we are not fully at home in this life, in our mortal bodies,
our earthly 'tents'.

At the heart of our Christian faith is a devotion to Jesus. From
the moment we first embark on the life of faith, we are on a journey
of discovery about just who this Christ is, who is declared in the
scriptures, worshipped in our churches and discussed endlessly
in conversations, books, blogs and documentaries. Pushing past
all the expert voices, we instinctively know that this rabbi from
Galilee, who lived 2000 years ago, has something to say to us
today. What we know about him causes us to love him, to worship
him, and to seek to serve him. But what we find is that in our
loving, worshipping and serving we start to get to know him, even

though we may well go through phases of our lives when we can scarcely see, hear or feel his presence. Something about this Jesus of Nazareth draws us, and something about us yearns to be close to him. This is all part of our homing instinct, because at the heart of the matter of homecoming is a longing to be near Christ, for it is he, more than anyone, who loves us so perfectly. It is in his presence that we know we can be ourselves without fear or shame. It is in his presence that we reach our homing destination. We may never understand this, but as sure as the swallow soars above the hot deserts of the Sahara, beating her tired wings that push her towards her little nest in that Derbyshire field, so my spirit also takes flight in the long journey to my home in Christ. So yes, when the time comes, I am willing for them to write 'home with the Lord', for I think that will be the moment when I can say I am *fully* home. It will not be another home, or even really a different home, for the homes of this world are all part of it. At that point the longing will be over, and I will no longer be homesick.

And so my dream on that cool April night about a big house, a field and a daughter set me on an exploration which I think, in all honesty, I have only just begun. Writing this book has shown me that this theme of homecoming is more than my own story. We all have dreams; we all have our longings for home. As we get into this theme it can take us anywhere, whether it be experiences of personal integration, fresh expressions of church or political liberation. The territory is huge and the quest could well take us all our days. But I am persuaded now that this homing instinct within us is one worth paying attention to, and is one that can lead us into some of the richest areas of exploration. And so, with countless others down the generations, I find myself praying, 'Take my hand, precious Lord, lead me home.'

For reflection

*What does it mean for you that heaven is 'home'? As you reach the end of
this book, is there any aspect of home that you want to think more about?*

A homeland blessing

*When you find yourself in far-off desert lands
May you be given the ears to hear your inner self
And come to your senses.
May your adventure take you to that place
Where you, the beloved on the earth,
Voyage with the breeze of God
To dream and to dare,
Drawing others to the homeland of grace.*

Reuben's story (7)

I had imagined this moment every day of my life since my sister had left home. I had hoped against hope that she was alive, and that she was not suffering. I had prayed for her and longed to see her. Now here was Judith standing in front of me, saying my name as a question as if she was not quite convinced that I was her brother. In that blazing setting sun I grasped hold of her, unable to stop the sobbing, for my feelings were too strong. How long we held each other I don't know, but at some point we let go and stood back to talk, piecing together the much-cherished memories that had remained so alive in our minds. More than anything I felt guilt at not having supported her, not having gone in search of her, and believing my father's version of the story. And yet, here she was, looking radiant and somehow whole, apparently undamaged by her terrible experience.

'I'm sorry, I'm sorry...' was all I could say, until she stopped me, putting a gentle hand over my mouth. 'Come,' she said and we moved over to the wall where the Rabbi had been sitting. And in that mysterious twilight you get after a sunset, she told me her story. Yes, it was true, Johanan had forced himself upon her and, after the act, claimed she had seduced him. Even before this event, she had never particularly liked him, but afterwards she hated him for what he had done and wanted to leave him, but he said it was shameful to divorce, and they had to go through with the preparation for marriage. Then it became clear she was carrying a child. Our father found out that fateful night and was full of rage, believing Johanan and blaming Judith for bringing disgrace on the family. He insisted that she leave the household and never return, so that Johanan could get a divorce and find someone else. He worked the plan out quickly, and our mother, although distraught, did not dare oppose him.

The hardest thing, she said, was saying goodbye to me that day, and she had missed me more than anyone. When I heard this I could hardly bear it. She told me that, after leaving home, she travelled north, to Tyre, to a distant relative that her mother had told her about. This relative turned out to be a wonderfully kind woman who took her in and treated her as a daughter. She refused to be worried by what the neighbours thought, and she helped Judith give birth to a little boy, named Reuben after me. She settled there and made a living as a seamstress and it was last year, she said, that this very Rabbi from Nazareth travelled north into their neighbourhood. One of her friends had a little girl who was desperately ill. She was a Gentile, and yet this Rabbi spoke of a God who was far bigger than the Jewish rulebooks we had grown up with and he healed that little girl. Everyone was amazed. Reuben immediately adored this man and sat at his feet listening to his stories.

I listened with astonishment as my sister told me how the Rabbi said he had to travel to Jerusalem, and invited others to travel with him. She said how she and Reuben knew they wanted to follow him, even though she became more and more fearful as they approached their home town. She looked straight at me as she told me this part of the story, her right hand squeezing her left as the memory brought back the feeling.

'One evening I went to the Rabbi to tell him the story of

my father and Johanan. I felt I had to tell him, and I felt that once he knew about me, he would not want me and Reuben to follow him. We would bring disgrace upon him. I had kept my feelings hidden for many years, but that night I howled out my pain and anger to the poor man. Do you know what he did? He reached out his hands and cupped my face in them, and said "Daughter, be released and be healed." For the first time in 15 years, a man called me "daughter". In that time I had believed I was not worthy to be a daughter. But here was the one we believe to be the Son of God looking me in the eye and calling me just that! For the first time in all those troubled years, I felt at peace. And when he said the words "be released", I felt every bit of that resentment and hatred towards Johanan and our father drain out of me. I have forgiven them. And when he said, "Be healed", oh Reuben, I was. I am! That is why I can be back in this town. I am no longer ashamed or afraid.'

Once again I had no words, but eventually I asked, 'And little Reuben?'

'Oh yes,' said Judith smiling, 'your nephew. He's not so little now. Look…', and she pointed to where the Rabbi was standing with a small group of people. 'That tall young man with his back to us. That is him. He says he never wants to leave the Rabbi's side, and somehow I don't think he will.'

Most people had now drifted off to their homes. Shemaiah had gone, and goodness only knows what he thought as he saw me hugging a strange woman. None of that mattered. I breathed in deeply and smelt the sweet fragrance of the ripening figs and felt the refreshing evening breeze fill my lungs. I was holding my sister's hand. In the last hour I had been found in my far-off land. I had come to myself, and had discovered that the Almighty was a Father who loved me, forgave me and even held a party for me. I am still a long way from feeling as forgiving as my sister, but perhaps, if I listen to a few more stories from this Rabbi, I might find a way.

I looked at my sister with her gentle eyes and said, 'Judith, I want to meet my nephew, and I want you to meet my wife, Ruth. I know she will love you. I want you both to come and live with us.' Judith fell towards me and again we held on tight to one another.

'Judith,' I said, pulling away from her.

'Yes, Reuben.'

'Have you or Reuben ever been to Crete?'

'To Crete? Why Crete?'

'Well, it's to do with my sandals,' I said and laughed in a way that I had not known since we ran through the fields together in the carefree days of our childhood.

As darkness fell the Rabbi sat again on the wall by the fig tree. The old stones were still warm from the afternoon sun, and he leant against the soft bark of the tree. 'Goodnight, Rabbi,' said his young friend Reuben, who skipped off and squeezed himself between his mother and his newfound uncle. The Rabbi smiled as he listened to our laughter and watched the three of us making our way home.

❖

Appendix

The following poem is by Trevor Hicks, my good friend and the Canon Poet of the Diocese of Derby. He wrote this prayer for the service for my commissioning by the Bishop of Derby into my freelance ministry. I am most grateful to him for allowing me to reproduce his poem here.[49]

Home

What storms I have travelled in dark light,
When high places, bleeding with red rains,
Transfused the ruptured veins of earth
With life ground from stones and
Trees and the vital breath of human clay
Once inert, but moving to be
One with all it ever was and
Is and shall be, then
To be for ever gone.

But I am not gone.
I am in and on this flow of life,
Washed in the running of tide on tide
Clothed in the glistening wrack and
Lichened cloths of hanging shores.
I am home from the pit and the mill
And the high country, with the sea
My pen and the sky an open page.

A strange, familiar place;
Known to me from distant
Glimmerings of infant dawns,
Hazed on far horizons of my mind,
Fresh Canaan of the honeyed stream,
Where waters mark my meeting with
A restless God.

Notes

1   Sister Stanislaus Kennedy, *Now is the Time*, expanded edition (Townhouse, 2006) pp. 139f.

2   Rowland Evans has published *My Sea is Wide* (Sunpenny Publishing, 2009), in which he writes about his feelings about becoming 70 and his experience in China.

3   The *Guardian*, 9 September 2008.

4   Sister Stanislaus Kennedy, *Gardening the Soul* (Simon&Schuster/Townhouse, 2001), reading for 25 December.

5   Frederick Buechner, *The Longing for Home* (HarperSanFrancisco, 1996), pp. 7–8.

6   John Betjeman, *Summoned By Bells* (John Murray, 1960, 1976), pp. 4–5.

7   John O'Donohue, *Benedictus* (Bantam Press, 2007), p. 99.

8   Sister Stanislaus, *Gardening the Soul*, p. 137.

9   Frederick Buechner, *The Yellow Leaves* (Westminster John Knox Press, 2008) p. 61.

10 I can't trace where this quote originally appears, but it is one of the first of his quotes to appear on any website search.

11 D. Bonhoeffer, *Letters and Papers from Prison*, English translation, 3rd edition (SCM, 1973), pp. 347f.

12 Frederick Buechner, *Now and Then* (HarperSanFrancisco, 1983), p. 99.

13 Transactional analysis is an integrative approach to understanding human behaviour. It was developed by Canadian-born US psychiatrist Eric Berne during the late 1950s.

14 Evans, *My Sea is Wide*.

15 Evans, *My Sea is Wide*, p. 33.

16 Gordon Mursell, *Praying in Exile* (DLT, 2005), pp. 1f.

17 Fiona Gardner, *Journeying Home* (DLT, 2004), p. 139.

18 Kenneth E. Bailey, *Poet and Peasant and Through Peasant Eyes*, combined edition (Eerdmans, 1983), pp. 142ff. Kenneth Bailey was Chairman of the Biblical Department at the Near Eastern School of Theology, Beirut.

19 Bailey, *Poet and Peasant and Through Peasant Eyes*, pp. 160–161.

20 Bailey, *Poet and Peasant and Through Peasant Eyes*, pp. 160–161.

21 David Adam, *Living in Two Kingdoms* (SPCK, 2007), p. xxiv.

22 Bailey, *Poet and Peasant and Through Peasant Eyes*, pp. 161–162.

23 Henri Nouwen, *The Return of the Prodigal Son* (DLT, 1994), p. 37.

24 Nouwen, *The Return of the Prodigal Son*, p. 39.

25 Buechner, *Now and Then*, p. 87.

26 Clare Nonhebel, *Far From Home* (Lion, 1999), p. 7.
27 Nonhebel, *Far From Home*, p. 10.
28 Walter Brueggemann, *Hopeful Imagination* (Fortress Press, 1986).
29 Brueggemann, *Hopeful Imagination*, p. 130.
30 This and the speeches that follow are based on Isaiah 40.
31 Walter Brueggemann, *Cadences of Home* (Westminster John Knox Press, 1997), p. 14.
32 Buechner, *Longing for Home*, p. 25.
33 Buechner, *Longing for Home*, p. 28.
34 Adam, *Living in Two Kingdoms*, p. 35.
35 Brueggemann, *Hopeful Imagination* Part 1, pp. 9–48.
36 Gerald A. Arbuckle, *Grieving for Change* (Geoffrey Chapman, 1991), p. 1.
37 Brueggemann, *Hopeful Imagination*, p. 34.
38 John Betjeman, *Summoned by Bells*, pp. 86–87.
39 Brueggemann, *Cadences of Home*, p. 115.
40 Walter Brueggemann, *Deep Memory, Exuberant Hope* (Fortress Press, 1999), p. 67.
41 Adrian Plass, 'Heaven', in Phil Baggaley et al., *City of Gold* (1997).
42 Buechner, *Longing for Home*, p. 21.
43 Buechner, *Longing for Home*, p. 23.
44 Stewart Henderson, *A Giant's Scrapbook* (Spire, 1989). The ten poems are at the beginning of the book.
45 Christopher Bryant, *The River Within* (DLT, 1978), p. 73.
46 C.S. Lewis, *The Last Battle* (Puffin Books, 1956), p. 155.
47 From an article by Ed Pilkington, *The Guardian* (3 April 2008).
48 Buechner, *Longing for Home*, p. 140.
49 Trevor Hicks, *In Western Light* (ISPCK, 2011), p. 41.

Pilgrimage

The journey to remembering our story

Andrew Jones

The age-old practice of pilgrimage is more popular than it has been for centuries. At a time when the Church seems increasingly exiled and estranged from our culture, more and more people are treading the ancient pilgrim routes, whether they are committed Christians, spiritual seekers or simply curious. The renewal of faith that they find on their journey often outweighs what happens in many churches.

Andrew Jones shows how pilgrimage can awaken those at all stages of belief to remembering the story of God's creating and redeeming work in history, which tells us who we are, where we have come from and where we are going. The act of remembering it not only offers a life-transforming way out of exile but points to the way home, to the place where we can live authentic and balanced lives. The book concludes with a focus on eight popular places of pilgrimage in the British Isles, drawing lessons from their history and spiritual heritage that can encourage and inspire us on our own faith journeys.

ISBN 978 1 84101 834 8   £8.99
Available from your local Christian bookshop or direct from BRF: visit www.brfonline.org.uk

Also from BRF

Rhythms of Grace

Finding intimacy with God in a busy life

Tony Horsfall

Rhythms of Grace emerges from a personal exploration of contemplative spirituality. Coming from an evangelical and charismatic background, Tony Horsfall felt an increasing desire to know God more deeply. At the same time, he felt an increasing dissatisfaction with his own spiritual life, as well as concern at the number of highly qualified and gifted people involved in Christian ministry who experience burn-out.

In this book he shows how contemplative spirituality, with its emphasis on realising our identity as God's beloved children and on being rather than doing, has vital lessons for us about discovering intimacy with God. It also provides essential insights about building a ministry that is both enjoyable and sustainable.

ISBN 978 1 84101 842 3   £7.99
Available from your local Christian bookshop or direct from BRF: visit www.brfonline.org.uk

Working from a Place of Rest

Jesus and the key to sustaining ministry

Tony Horsfall

Exhaustion, burnout, tiredness, even breakdown... sadly, such conditions are all too common these days, not least among those involved in some kind of Christian ministry, whether full-time, part-time or voluntary. In striving to do our utmost for God, we can easily forget that there were many times when Jesus himself was willing to rest, to do nothing except wait for the Spirit's prompting, so that he demonstrated the vital principle of 'working from a place of rest'.

Drawing on extensive experience of training and mentoring across the world, Tony Horsfall reflects on the story of Jesus and the Samaritan woman to draw out practical guidance for sustainable Christian life and work. As he writes: 'Come and sit by the well for a while. Take some time out to reflect on how you are living and working. Watch Jesus and see how he does it. Listen to what the Spirit may be saying to you deep within, at the centre of your being; and maybe, just maybe, God will give you some insights that will change your life and sustain your ministry over the long haul.'

ISBN 978 1 84101 544 6   £6.99

Available from your local Christian bookshop or direct from BRF: visit www.brfonline.org.uk

Simple Gifts

Blessings in disguise

Kevin Scully

We are familiar with the idea of friendship as a gift, something that bestows blessing on our lives. Hospitality enriches both giver and receiver, while humour is a gift that, used sensitively, can shed a warm light even on a bleak situation. There are other aspects of life that we may take for granted or even actively dislike—aspects such as ignorance, tears, grief and anger.

Drawing on scripture, song, poetry and insights from daily life, Kevin Scully considers different facets of ten such gifts, from the familiar to the unexpected. He shows how each has the potential to be a source of personal wonder and joy and can also draw us closer to God and to one another. *Simple Gifts* is a book that can be read from beginning to end or dipped into for reflection or inspiration.

ISBN 978 1 84101 851 5   £7.99
Available from your local Christian bookshop or direct from BRF: visit www.brfonline.org.uk

Also from BRF

Shaping the Heart

Reflections on spiritual formation and fruitfulness

Pamela Evans

God created the human heart to be a worship-filled, holy place with himself in residence, a garden in which the fruit of the Spirit may grow. *Shaping the Heart* is a book for every Christian who wants their heart to become—through the healing and redemptive touch of heavenly grace and mercy—a place where God delights to dwell.

Shaping the Heart is designed for practical use, whether as individual reading for a retreat or quiet day or for shared study and discussion in a group setting. The book considers different aspects of our lives in the light of Christian teaching and looks at how God can touch and transform us through his Spirit, so that we become fruitful disciples. Chapters conclude with three Bible reflections as a springboard to further prayer and reflection.

ISBN 978 1 84101 726 6   £7.99
Available from your local Christian bookshop or direct from BRF: visit www.brfonline.org.uk

Also from BRF

Discovering the Spiritual Exercises of Saint Ignatius

Larry Warner

This book is an adaptation of the Spiritual Exercises of St Ignatius Loyola, to help you to embark on a life-transforming journey toward Christlikeness. For nearly 500 years, the Exercises have been a tool for spiritual formation. During those years their popularity has ebbed and flowed, but they are now experiencing something of a revival across the breadth of the Church.

This is not a book about the methods or techniques of Christian formation but one that enables you to come before God through the Gospel narratives in order to encounter Jesus afresh. If you hunger for something deeper, yearn to walk with Jesus (not just read about him) and desire to embrace more of what God is doing in and through you, then this is the book for you.

ISBN 978 1 84101 883 6   £10.99
Available from your local Christian bookshop or direct from BRF: visit www.brfonline.org.uk

Also from BRF

Embracing Dusty Detours

A spiritual search for depth in desert places

Lynne E. Chandler

'I feel at last that I am embracing the present moment of life. I haven't arrived, I'm just resting; resting beside quiet waters that inevitably churn and stir from time to time and turn into strong currents that drag me back into the river of the hectic everyday.'

This book takes you on a quest through the bustling chaos of Middle Eastern city life and the drama of a youth-led revolution to endless stretches of desert sand and Bible places from Mount Sinai to the shores of Galilee. This quest, along life's dusty detours, is in search of oases of all kinds—people, places, and little glimpses of eternity. Lynne's journey involves laughter, tears and raw honesty, and is often one lurch forward and two steps backward, but it has led her to deeper insights into faith and greater reliance on God than she ever imagined.

ISBN 978 1 84101 829 4   £6.99
Available from your local Christian bookshop or direct from BRF: visit www.brfonline.org.uk

Enjoyed

this book?

Write a review—we'd love to hear what you think.
Email: reviews@brf.org.uk

Keep up to date—receive details of our new books as they happen.
Sign up for email news and select your interest groups at:
www.brfonline.org.uk/findoutmore/

Follow us on Twitter @brfonline

By post—to receive new title information by post (UK only), complete the form below and post to: BRF Mailing Lists, 15 The Chambers, Vineyard, Abingdon, Oxfordshire, OX14 3FE

Your Details
Name _____
Address_____
_____
Town/City _____ Post Code _____
Email_____

Your Interest Groups (*Please tick as appropriate)	
☐ Advent/Lent	☐ Messy Church
☐ Bible Reading & Study	☐ Pastoral
☐ Children's Books	☐ Prayer & Spirituality
☐ Discipleship	☐ Resources for Children's Church
☐ Leadership	☐ Resources for Schools

Support your local bookshop
Ask about their new title information schemes.